THE LANGUAGE OF MODERN POLITICS

By the same author

THE BUSINESSMAN IN PUBLIC
THE DICTIONARY OF DISEASED ENGLISH
THE JARGON OF THE PROFESSIONS
THE END OF GIN AND TONIC MAN: A FUTURE FOR PUBLIC RELATIONS

The Language of Modern Politics

Kenneth Hudson

'A good deal of deceit is essential to the proper working of any kind of institution' – K. R. Minogue, *The Liberal Mind*, 1963

© Kenneth Hudson 1978

All rights reserved. No part of this publication may be reproduced or transmitted, in any form or by any means, without permission

First edition 1978
First Published in Papermac 1980

Published by
THE MACMILLAN PRESS LTD
London and Basingstoke
Associated companies in Delhi
Dublin Hong Kong Johannesburg Lagos
Melbourne New York Singapore Tokyo

Printed in Great Britain by
Billing & Sons Ltd.,
Guildford, London and
Worcester

British Library Cataloguing in Publication Data

Hudson, Kenneth
 The language of modern politics
 1. Communication in politics 2. Sociolinguists
 1. Title
 320'.01'4   JA76

ISBN 0-333 21438-2 (HC)
ISBN 0-333 28361-9 (Papermac)

The paperback edition of this book is sold subject to the condition that it shall not, by way of trade or otherwise, be lent, resold, hired out, or otherwise circulated without the publisher's prior consent, in any form of binding or cover other than that in which it is published and without a similar condition including this condition being imposed on the subsequent purchaser

*This book is sold subject to the
standard conditions of the
Net Book Agreement*

Contents

Foreword vii

1 What politics is about 1
2 Product differentiation in politics 21
3 Getting and holding power 39
4 Language as group-cement 61
5 Today's political abuse 82
6 Politicians can be straightforward, sometimes 102
7 The real man behind the speechwriters 122
8 Government public relations 141

Notes 154
Books found useful 159
Index 163

Foreword

This book interprets 'modern politics' to mean 'politics of the Sixties and Seventies'. Most of the illustrative examples of political language have been drawn from this period and I have ventured outside it only when a comparison with earlier practice seemed likely to prove useful.

The base of operations has been Britain and British political life, but throughout the book I have used material from elsewhere, particularly the United States, where the danger of parochialism seemed to be becoming serious. Little that is said about the English-speaking countries would not also be applicable to other Western democracies, even if they have not been specifically named. The trends that have been observed are international, although the details and emphasis will vary from country to country.

Like George Orwell thirty years ago, I have found no reason to keep 'politics' in one compartment and 'language' in another. I believe, on the contrary, that the two are inseparable and that, whatever academic convention and etiquette may prefer, the public interest is best served by investigating a total situation, rather than by observing the dividing lines between 'disciplines'. I have no reason to be prejudiced against either Left or Right, and I have tried to judge their representatives by what they do and say, rather than from any preconceived standpoint. If politicians behave in a foolish or sinister manner, I am not responsible, whatever their creed or nationality.

I have no political ambitions and I have never taken part in any kind of political activity. I am an essentially non-political animal. Whether this makes me better or worse fitted to examine the way in which politicians express themselves is open to discussion. I should have thought myself that this is a field in which independence is very much a virtue.

K. H.

1 What Politics is about

'Politics' is not an easy word to use, mainly because it means such different things to different people. One recalls the days, not entirely past, when, to the Presidents of many Women's Institutes in rural areas of Britain, Conservative politics were not politics at all. To hold Conservative views was as natural as breathing and eating, so natural and God-given, indeed, that the rule about no politics or religion at Institute meetings was assumed to apply only to the introduction of socialist ideas into the peaceful Wednesday evening atmosphere. 'Politics', in this sense and context, was almost synonymous with controversy and disturbance of the peace, a distasteful and antisocial activity, a piece of bad manners. There probably had to be politicians and politics, in the same way as there had to be drains, slaughterhouses and public hangmen, but it was better to keep them safely in the background, as unpleasant necessities, operated by insensitive professionals. At General Elections politics burst through to the surface for a short time, rather like a volcano erupting, but the turbulence was soon over and normal people could then forget about politics for another five years or so. The poor might complain about their lot and the unemployed might emerge from their ghettoes and march to Hyde Park or the House of Commons, but that sort of thing could be kept under control. The left-wing politicians, who were always demanding a new order of society, in which there would be no poor and no unemployed and where those who did not work did not eat, might be noisy and rude, but they were not dangerous and one could, for the most part, disregard them.

This very widespread middle-class attitude miraculously survived the 1914–18 War to an extent one would hardly have thought possible, but, since the British General Strike of 1929, since the Nazis came to power in Germany, and since the rise of the Soviet Union to the position of one of the two great world powers, politics in the Western democracies has ceased to be either a form of self-indulgence or a wholly professional activity. It has permeated every aspect of life, made it essential for the ordinary citizen everywhere to learn new ways of defending himself, and produced real and imaginary social divisions which were not obvious or particularly troublesome before. The definition of politics has, inevitably, undergone subtle but considerable changes in the process.

The *Oxford English Dictionary* was last revised, so far as the letter P is concerned, in the early 1930s, that is, when Nazism and Stalinism were still in their infancy and before the Second World War and the struggles for world power and national independence which came after it, events which transformed the relations between people and their rulers. At this time, 1933, with Hitler a year in the saddle, the *Oxford English Dictionary* offered four meanings for the world 'politics'. Two are concerned with politics as an activity, and two with politics as an object of study and analysis.

On the activity side, we are given:

'Political actions or practice' and
'Political affairs or business; political life'

Passively and philosophically, it is:

'The science and art of government; the science dealing with the form, organisation, and administration of a state or part of one, and with the regulation of its relations with other states' and
'The political principles, convictions, opinions or sympathies of a person or party.'

This amounts to saying that politics is both a theory, a science, and a technology. The scientists and the technologists do not always like or understand one another. Lord George-Brown once made the point in a characteristically blunt way: 'You are,' he said in the course of a television interview, 'a logical thinker as far as logic will take you, but there comes a point when logic won't take you any further. That is when you have to work it out for yourself, and something that is instinctive tells you where to take it from there. This is why the academics get it wrong in the end; they have got all the knowledge, but God forgot to give them mechanics for understanding and turning the logic into action.'[1]

By this, the former Labour Foreign Secretary meant that intelligent humanity is divided into two groups, the thinkers and analysts – the 'academics' – and the doers, each of which tends to mistrust and possibly despise the other for its supposed inadequacies. The doers, with whom Lord George-Brown identified himself, are apt to become annoyed with the thinkers for what appears to be their wilful refusal to dirty their hands and souls with the practical work that has to be done if society is to be made to function. The thinkers, on the other hand, find it extremely difficult, even repugnant, to make the compromises and tell the lies and half-truths which are demanded of them if theory is to be translated into action. So the 'academics', like the Women's Institute Presidents of old, are intensely and fundamentally suspicious of mere 'politicians', and the 'politicians' show a corresponding degree of scorn for 'intellectuals'. Occasionally, an 'academic' will decide to cross the fence and take part in the hurly-burly of politics. If he does, and if he makes a success of the venture, it will be for reasons of ambition and longing for power, proving that he was not a true academic at heart. If, having tasted it, he finds politics, either the national or the local brand, unpleasant he will return whence he came and prove Lord George-Brown's point, that stamina and success in politics is a matter of temperament. Not everyone is born to work in a slaughterhouse, carry out executions, or keep the sewage disposal plant in good working order.

Geoffrey K. Roberts has produced a definition of 'politics' which reflects today's moods and perplexities very well.

'*Politics* The word refers both to an activity and to the study of that activity. As an activity, politics is the process in a social system – not necessarily confined to the level of the national state – by which the goals of that system are selected, ordered in terms of priority, both temporarily and concerning resource allocation, and implemented. It thus involves both co-operation and a resolution of conflict by means of the exercise of political authority and if necessary coercion. Politics usually involves the activities of groups of various kinds, including groups of a specifically political type such as political parties. It is distinguished from other social processes by its concern with the 'public' goals of society, whereas economics may be concerned with public or private allocations of resources and social processes of a non-political nature with non-public activities.'[2]

The excellent dictionary of politics from which this key definition is taken deals with the difficult words, those which are surrounded with argument and controversy. As its author rightly points out, unless one arrives at a fairly exact agreement as to the meaning of these words, no worthwhile analysis or discussion is possible. He has consequently wrestled, on behalf of both himself and his readers, with such emotionally-loaded terms as capitalism, élite, Marxism, communism, revolution and socialism, in an attempt to reach objective definitions which have some chance of general acceptance, even by those whose approach to politics is highly partisan. In this he succeeds as well as anyone could hope to succeed in today's climate of hatred, prejudice and violence, in which neutrality and impartiality are not widely regarded as virtues.

Given that objective definitions are possible or desirable, an assumption with which, unfortunately, not everyone would agree, it is difficult to improve on what Mr. Roberts has to say about the four explosive terms, Capitalism, Communism, Marxism and Socialism.

CAPITALISM: defined as 'The economic system in which the greater part of the economy is controlled by private, i.e. non-state owners, relying on the private provision of capital investment in return for distributed profits. Its proponents believe that such a system tends to maximise the satisfaction of economic needs by providing for the most rational distribution of economic resources.'

COMMUNISM: 'An ideology based on the communal ownership of all property, coupled with some form of non-hierarchical political structure. In consequence the social structure would be classless, money would be abolished and work would be directed by and performed willingly in the interests of the community as a whole: "From each according to his ability to each according to his needs". Except in the particular context of Marxist doctrine, communism is thus one form of socialism, differing from other forms primarily in its emphasis on social and economic change as a preliminary condition of political change rather than as a consequence of it.'

MARXISM: 'The system of thought regarding the interrelationships of history, economics, politics and social life based on the writings of Karl Marx, particularly in the communist manifesto and *Das Kapital*.'

SOCIALISM: 'An ideology based on the belief that the means of production in a society should be owned and controlled by the community, that the purpose of productive enterprise should be the satisfaction of communal rather than individual needs, and that individual fulfilment can only be realised when communal needs have been satisfied. Such goals imply political as well as economic changes in a society.'

But Geoffrey Roberts, like all dictionary-makers and explainers, cannot produce definitions in a vacuum. The words he uses and the habits of mind he reflects are those of his own time. In saying that politics 'refers both to an activity and to the study of that activity' he is doing no more than paraphrase the *OED* entry of 40 years earlier. The *OED* would not, however, have talked about a 'process in a social system' or 'resource allocation' or 'the public goals of society'. This was not the language of the Twenties and Thirties; it is almost inescapable today.

Change works both ways. There are words which were in the normal vocabulary of both politicians and writers on politics half a century ago and which are heard much less today. It is both curious and sad, for instance, that the very well-known book edited by Professor Richard Rose, *Politics in England Today*, first published in 1974, does not have in its index, 'propaganda', 'lie', 'deception', or 'half-truth', all of which figure as prominently in the English political scene now as they did a generation or so ago.

If, however, one accepts Geoffrey Roberts' definition of politics – and is not easy to imagine finding a better one – two major important questions immediately arise. The first is: 'Do all the major parties see the business, aims and satisfactions of politics in the same way?' 'Do they all see the same possibilities in this abstraction called politics?' The second is: 'Are there really only two political roles, that of the activist, the professional political animal, on the one hand, and of the student, the analyser, on the other?'

All political parties issue programmes, stating their aims and indicating why these aims and the methods chosen to achieve them are worthy of public support. In preparing their manifestoes, all parties make certain assumptions, probably correctly. Most people are reckoned to want peace, work and enough money to allow them to live in what, given contemporary ambitions, they consider to be reasonable comfort, most people regard war, unemployment and poverty as major evils. All parties therefore stress that to vote for them is to make peace and prosperity more certain, while to vote for their opponents is to bring war and economic depression closer.

This is safe ground. Much more dangerous, however, is any attempt to put into words what the party leaders and theoreticians really think about human nature. They certainly have hypotheses about what men's main motives are and, equally important, may be, if skilfully directed and channelled. These views are unlikely to flatter the people who are being wooed as supporters and they must consequently never be released in any but the most sweetened and diluted form. Brutally, however, the different party views on political motivation might be summarised in something like the following way.

The Socialists assume that the majority of human beings are driven by feelings of envy. All but the most saintly and altruistic characters are embittered and enraged by the knowledge that some people, possibly many people, are better off than they are. It is the differential, other people's relative advantage, which is intolerable. One can put up with austerity, shortages and misery, even take a masochistic pleasure in them, provided one can be sure that everyone else is equally deprived and wretched: what is intolerable is that there should be exceptions to the general penury, absence of opportunity or amenity, or whatever the current lack is seen to be. So, in wartime, there is an almost murderous hatred of farmers, blackmarketeers, and people with prudently accumulated stocks of tinned food; and, in peace-time, an equal frenzy against grammar schools and private medical treatment.

The Conservatives assume, but never, sober, say, that most of their fellow-citizens are actuated by greed and by a never-ending desire to add to their possessions. The mainspring of all human activity is what is politely called competition, that is, the attempt to acquire more possessions or more expensive and desirable possessions than one's friends and neighbours. The State, so the Conservative credo goes, will prosper to the extent that competition between individuals or organisations is not restricted or discouraged. If people's chances, or what they regard as their chances, of getting more than their neighbours are deliberately limited or circumscribed in any way, they will stop working hard and the community as a whole will be impoverished. The public good depends on unfettered competition between individuals. Greed is a universal motive, competition is the primary rule of life.

The individual, like the individual business, must, of course, be allowed to keep a sufficiently large proportion of the income resulting from his labours. The re-distribution of wealth through taxation harms the community by discouraging the most energetic and creative members. Provided that each individual gets all or nearly all the profits from his own work, there is no limit to how hard he will work or to how much he will produce.

The Fascists, by whatever name, base their tactics and their policy on a different but, as one might think, equally unworthy and degrading assumption. They believe that the majority of people suffer from chronic status-anxiety, from an obsessive fear that they or the group with which they identify themselves are not receiving the social respect to which they believe they are entitled. Given this anxiety, they will naturally wish to discover and conquer the hostile forces – Jews, freemasons, blacks, Welshmen, or whoever – which have been preventing them from getting their proper due. Since their own worth is never in question, the lack of regard shown to them can only be due to the machinations of evil-minded enemies.

The Communists would make the same basic assumptions as the Socialists, but with the important addition that history has to be interpreted as a continuous conflict between the present holders of power, who wish to retain and increase that power, and those who wish to defeat and replace them. In the Marxist view, power does not have to be justified. It is considered an absolute good by the most able members of society. Able people naturally want power; to abandon it is always a sign of weakness or degeneracy.

It is probable that those who decide on a political career have a desire for power which is considerably above the average. In a liberal democracy, this is usually kept under control and society does not suffer unduly. Under a one-party dictatorial régime, on the other hand, the situation is very different. What has happened in the Soviet Union during the 60 years of Communist power has been accurately and succinctly described by Bertrand Russell.

'Power,' he notes, neither approvingly nor disapprovingly, 'is sweet: it is a drug, the desire for which increases with habit. Those who have seized power, even for the noblest of motives, soon persuade themselves that there are good reasons for not relinquishing it. This is particularly likely to happen if they believe themselves to represent some immensely important cause. They will feel that their opponents are ignorant and perverse; before long, they will come to hate them. What right have these wretches to oppose the coming of the millenium? If they have to be persecuted, no doubt that is regrettable, but, after all, you can't make an omelette without breaking eggs. Meanwhile the pioneers, having established an oligarchy, are succeeded in their privileged position by men of more ordinary clay, who like the privileges but are not much interested in the millenium. For these new men, the important thing is to keep their power, not to use it as a means to an eventual paradise. And so what were means become ends, and the original ends are forgotten, except on Sundays. It is an old story, and should be a familiar one, and yet Lenin and his admirers failed to draw the moral.'[3]

No Soviet official in a leading position has ever analysed the situation in this way, at any rate in public, but Bertrand Russell's interpretation fits the facts and it explains the fundamental assumption behind the Communist theory of the dictatorship, that ultimate success in achieving the goal is so certain as to justify the condemnation of generations of Soviet citizens to medieval restrictions on their liberty and on their freedom of thought and expression. Our Russian children must be protected until the last capitalist wolf has been tracked down and exterminated.

Similarly, no British Socialist would ever insist in so many plain words that most people's lives are ruled by envy, no Conservative would say that greed makes the world go round, and no Fascist would want to put his name to the theory that the world is peopled by pathetic little men longing to be regarded as big men. Broadly speaking, assumptions about human motivation are not publishable, at least by those actively engaged in the political game, whereas 'principles', being flexible and easily modified as required, are always on-stage material. It may well be left to the students and observers of politics, however, to deduce the principles and the theory behind the action, which is another way of saying that the political parties cannot escape the intellectuals, hard as they may try and embarrassing as intellectuals may often be.

Practical politicians, especially in the English-speaking world, may deny on occasion that there is any theory behind their actions. They may claim, as Lord George-Brown has done, that they proceed largely by instinct, pragmatic step by pragmatic step. Or, like the English Conservative, Sir Ian Gilmour, they may choose to make a virtue out of necessity and to say that there is no such thing as Conservative theory, because Conservatives, unlike their woolly-minded opponents on the Left, hate abstractions.[4] This, as the *Spectator*'s experienced and suitably hard-boiled political correspondent, Alan Watkins, has remarked, is 'reminiscent of Morrison's observation that socialism is what the Labour Government does; likewise of Mrs. Castle's conference-cry in the days when she was a minister: "Do you think I, Barbara Castle, would be doing this if it wasn't socialist?" [5]

This brings us to the second question raised above, as to whether there really are only two troupes of political performers, the politicians and the analysts. Is any definition of politics which suggests this sufficiently comprehensive? How, for instance, is one to label the full-time television interviewer of the type of Britain's Robin Day, whose whole working life, and for all one knows and suspects, his non-working life, too, is spent among politicians, gossipping with them, prodding them, arguing with them, encouraging them and functioning as their public memory? A person in Day's position produces no opinions of his own on the topics and people that provide him with his daily bread, although he is known to have been a Liberal candidate for Parliament many years ago and may quite possibly still hold Liberal views, whatever these may be. Day is that rather rare person, the wholly political animal, the man who lives and breathes politics and who never appears to find them boring. He is not a political analyst, in the sense that he takes a cool, detached view of what the gladiators are doing down below in the arena and then presents the public with a coherent, penetrating view of it all. He exists in order to prod the politicians and make them talk, to remind them of things they have said in the past and to ask them to explain their actions and utterances. He is an essential part of their world, sufficiently fair and friendly to persuade even the grandest of figures to sit in the studio with him, yet sufficiently omniscient and well-informed to make most of them slightly wary and even frightened of him. He is obviously not an academic, nor is he the usual kind of political journalist. He is not a reporter, yet to describe him as a political interviewer seems slightly insulting. What is he?

The best way of answering this may be to return to Lord George-Brown's point. Does Robin Day belong to those of whom it can be said that 'they have all the knowledge, but God forgot to give them mechanics for understanding and turning the logic into action'? Is he trying to make the system work a little better, to keep politicians up to the mark in the public interest? Is he, in political terms, a scientist or a technologist? Is he living out some kind of fantasy life, as a Member of Parliament manqué?

The point is an important one – and Day is not, of course, the only person to whom it relates – because this type of middleman in politics has a considerable influence on the way in which politicians learn to present themselves to the public. They will be coached and disciplined to be more straightforward and intelligible than their professional instincts would normally consider prudent. From time to time they will be invited or instructed to translate a particularly obscure piece of jargon and to give a plain answer to a plain question. Some, inevitably, will do this more willingly and more successfully than others. But, in most cases, it will not be a one-way process. The Days – it is permissible to use the name as a generic term for a special breed of animal – will play give and take with the people they are interviewing. Situated as they are on a not uncomfortable broadcasting fence, they will, for a lot of the time, talk the politicians' language in order to make them feel that they are in friendly, understanding company. Even if the intention is to lead the victim to the place of crucifixion and then to drive in the nails and hoist the cross, the prelude is likely to be gentle and reassuring. Like will be talking to like, one old political horse will be munching oats with another.

The journalist who writes *about* politicians and politics is in quite a different position. He is watching the wild animals at play, writing from the safety and detachment of the other side of the bars. The Days are actually in the cage, frolicking, grunting and sometimes snarling with them. It is entirely possible, of course, to have more of politicians' company than is good for one's personal or professional health. Overmuch cameraderie and day-to-day mixing with politicians can weaken one's ability to view their actions and sayings objectively. The shrewdest and most effect critics of the political scene have tended to be people, like Jonathan Swift and George Orwell, for whom politics was only a part of life, people whose values had been formed and strengthened outside politics.

As an example of this, one can consider a biting attack made by Bernard Levin in the autumn of 1976 on the Chancellor of the Exchequer, and published in *The Times*,[6] where Mr. Levin is the resident scourge of public figures everywhere whose conduct seems worthy of penetrating comment. Using the kind of robust, incisive language which has made him the highest paid journalist in Britain, Mr. Levin goes first for the Chancellor, noting that 'it used to be said that one should never trust a man who hunts south of the Thames, a man with a waxed moustache, or a man who eats soup at lunch, and we can now add to this trio of rubrics for the infallible detection of bounders a man who calls a loan a standby credit'. He observes that, against all the evidence, Mr. Healey had forecast an economic growth rate of 5 per cent over the next three years, with the figure as high as 7.5 per cent in the manufacturing sector, and had declared that the Government had been 'conspicuously successful in controlling the money supply', that its policies 'have contributed to a massive strengthening of our economy' and that inflation 'could be down to as low as 7 per cent by the end of next year'. Having unburdened himself of these prophecies, the Chancellor had gone on to say: 'I think it would be quite helpful if commentators took as robust and patriotic a view of the situation as the ordinary working people of this country do. Confidence is the name of the game, and we do not want people sapping it.'

Bernard Levin, rightly considering himself to be one of the commentators who had incurred the Chancellor's displeasure, went into the attack. Mr. Healey, he said, 'wishes the commentators to take the same admiring view of him and his activities that " the ordinary working people" do. To put it another way, he wants the commentators to believe the endless parade of grubby mendacities with which, for years now, those who govern us have sought to govern our attention from mendacity.' In Mr. Levin's view, 'the truth, of course, is that Mr. Healey knew perfectly well all along that such few "ordinary people" as still believed the rubbish he was talking were being most cruelly deceived, and that the awakening that they would all too soon experience would be more cruel still'.

In the West, politics includes, as it certainly does not in the socialist, or for that matter, in most of the developing countries, this kind of attack on Ministers. In accepting the role of 'commentator' on the political scene, Bernard Levin clearly believes that he has a public duty to expose fraud and hypocrisy, in both high and low places. To allow him to do this as effectively as possible, he maintains a formidable private card index of statements made by people prominent in public life. With the help of his remarkable memory, these quotations can be produced at the right moment in order to damn and embarrass the unfortunate culprits. It is this unceasing monitoring of their activities which causes politicians both at home and abroad to go in daily fear of Mr. Levin. The Russian Government in particular has good reason to regard him as its Number One enemy in Britain. But – and the point is an important one – he can hardly be regarded as a political analyst, or as a student of politics, in the ordinary sense of these terms. He is meticulous and infinitely painstaking, but he does not have an academic cast of mind. He is not content to sift the evidence in order to produce theories and models. He believes there are false gods to be toppled, shams to be exposed, and rogues and tyrants to be denounced and he uses the printed word as his weapon for this purpose. The *Washington Post* journalists who discovered the facts of the Watergate scandal and who helped to rid the United States of the President involved were cast in the same mould.

Robin Day, Bernard Levin and the *Washington Post* are an integral part of politics, as Western countries understand it. Politicians in these countries may often wish that such people, or some of them, did not exist, but as things stand at the moment they are an essential and valuable part of the system. How valuable one comes to realise only by studying the workings of politics in those countries of the world – the majority – in which criticism of those in positions of power is not tolerated at all. Political figures in the Soviet Union, Argentina or South Africa do not welcome advice from journalists or television commentators, however expert and well-informed these people may be. 'Politics', in Western countries, includes the dimension of criticism; elsewhere, however much public talk there may be about 'democracy', politics means little more than getting and holding power and in such a situation criticism of any kind is likely to be as well received as a blow-lamp in an ice-cream factory. A Russian Bernard Levin is hardly conceivable, except in exile.

A major difficulty, even in the 'easy' conditions of the West, is that so few people, even highly intelligent people, appear to understand that politics has no values of its own at all. When journalists or moralists or philosophers attempt to remind politicians of such concepts as lying, unscrupulousness, faulty memory or failure to comprehend logic, they are committed to the impossible. Nothing is valued in politics unless it is believed to be useful as a means of keeping a stronger grip on power or of embarrassing or defeating one's opponents. This is well understood by all politicians everywhere. In this respect, there is no difference whatever between a Russian minister and a British or Norwegian minister. Yet the British minister cannot get away easily with the kind of actions and statements which are taken for granted in Russia. The reason for this has been well analysed by K. R. Minogue.

'The differences between regimes in the amount of lying, deceit, fraud and illusion must be attributed,' he says, 'not to political variations, but to the moral character of the regime. Certain ways of life, notably those of Western Europe, are capable of generating institutions (such as the press, an opposition, free universities) which lessen the advantages of deceit.'[7] Put more bluntly, this means that in the West lying politicians always run the risk of being found out and pilloried for their misdeeds. Such a fate is not automatic, but it is always there as a possibility. The prudent minister or senator, or whoever he may be, will ask himself if the lie or the unjustified accusation is really worth it. Dare he gamble on the loss of face, the tarnishing of his public image, which a skilful, observant critic might well bring about?

Such a question implies, of course, that the person in question is aware that he is talking nonsense, possibly dangerous or wicked nonsense. This is not necessarily the case. He may have lived for a long time in a fantasy world, hedged about with ideology and dogma, which has destroyed his ability to react to words in a way which a non-political animal would consider normal. An ideology is essentially a set of beliefs which cannot and must not be questioned. It is buttressed by dogmas, and, indeed, depends on them for its existence and survival. One cannot argue with an ideology, because the answers one receives will always be in terms of the ideology. One's queries and accusations bounce back from a foam-rubber wall. The politician soaked in ideology has long passed the point at which he can engage in anything that could be called rational discussion.

When a politician asks himself, 'Should I do this or that?' he is not necessarily or even probably posing a moral question. He does not mean, 'Is it ethically right that I should do this?' Almost certainly he means, 'Is it strategically wise that I should take this step, make this decision, at this particular moment?' In nine cases out of ten, the politician's should is not the plain man's should, or, for that matter, the lawyer's should. It is only for a very brief and possibly transitory period that there has been any doubt in the matter. During the seventeenth and eighteenth centuries – one is speaking here of Britain – the feeling grew, as the essence of a liberal philosophy, that all actions must have a moral basis. Politics came to be regarded as a means towards a society which would be, in the strictly moral sense, better. To many people, brought up in the liberal tradition and powerfully influenced by it, this is how politics still appears, a tool, a means to a desirable end, a way of improving the human condition. This being so, the question of, for instance, whether people should be expected to meet all or some of the cost of their medical treatment, should be capable of being decided or at least discussed rationally. In practice, however, a deeply entrenched dogma within the British Labour Party is that all medical treatment should be free. Anyone saying or thinking otherwise is automatically branded as a dangerous Tory reactionary. The case for some form of payment is consequently never explored, and so it is with other key dogmas, such as Full Employment, the Right to Strike, the Right to Peaceful Picketing, the Right to Work, and the rest.

Morally, the Trade Union closed shop may be indefensible and so indeed it was held to be until very recently. What has changed has not been the logic of the situation – the arguments for the closed shop are no better and no worse than they were 20 or 50 years ago – but the power of trade unionism. The Labour Party, especially when in power, has to follow public opinion in the matter with great sensitivity. If it were, for instance, to show little sympathy with a body of men striking to force a closed shop at their place of work or to toughen and enforce the law with regard to picketing, it would be doing so for entirely political reasons, from an anxiety to avoid a course of action which would endanger votes or other tokens of public support. Any question of morality, of right or wrong, would be seen by the party managers as completely irrelevant. The point at issue would be simply, is this or that course of action more likely to win or lose us votes?

There are those who may feel that such a view is unnecessarily cynical. Is there no place in modern politics, they may ask, for men and women with ideals, public-spirited people with good causes to support? One has to try to distinguish between causes and vested interests, and it is never easy to do this. A Member of Parliament or Congressman may believe passionately that his fellow-citizens would enjoy better health if they were vegetarians or if they could be persuaded to get out of their motorcars and ride bicycles, and he may seize every possible opportunity to propagate such views. In such cases, his views are undoubtedly likely to carry more conviction if he has no financial interest in the supply of lentils and soya-beans or in the manufacture of bicycles. Many people active in both national and local politics do certainly use their position in order to advance this or that sectional interest, and probably no great harm is done if their business connections are well-known, since both their immediate audience and the public will make the necessary allowances. It is, in any case, very useful, in any political assembly or organisation, to have a good mixture of occupations and expert knowledge available.

This is not, however, the most important point. Suppose a Member of Parliament should decide to espouse the cause of thalidomide babies or workers who have developed cancer as a result of contact with asbestos, demanding public enquiries, financial compensation and other action which may be required if justice is to be done to the victims. He may be utterly sincere in his views and his campaigning, but he cannot avoid gaining considerable political advantage as a result of publicity for what he is doing. Whether he has this aim in mind at the outset, who can say? Were those nineteenth century Members of Parliament who pressed for the abolition of the Corn Laws, slavery and the employment of children in factories entirely altruistic and disinterested? Did the thought of votes and prestige never occur to them?

If the cause is likely to be popular, one's suspicions are likely to be more easily aroused. Where, however, the politician is pushing for legislation or action which is, at the time, unfashionable, it is fair to assume that it is conviction and conscience, rather than a desire for popularity, which is motivating him. The abolition of the death penalty, the easing of penalties imposed on homosexuals, the ending of the Vietnam War are cases in point. It is not, alas, always true that sincerity and single-mindedness shine through a man's public behaviour. Would that it were so.

Even more difficult to analyse and evaluate is the behaviour of the fanatic and doctrinaire. If, for example, a politician refers, perhaps with great strength of feeling, to such concepts as 'social justice', 'the redistribution of wealth', 'equality of opportunity', or 'The American way of life', is one to conclude that he has thought deeply about those matters or that he is merely using phrases which will commend him to his party and to the electorate? Worse still, how is one to differentiate between two members of the same party in the same legislature and debating chamber, one of whom is talking about, say, 'the redistribution of wealth' like a parrot or a ventriloquist's dummy, and the other who is using what is to him a carefully chosen and considered expression of deep thought and feeling? In politics, as in any branch of human activity, one person's cliché is another's profundity. When in doubt, however, it is always safer to conclude that the cliché is what one is being offered.

Why, after all, do politicians talk at all, at any rate in public? Is it to explain, to teach, to persuade, to charm, to quarrel, to obstruct, to ridicule, to demolish or simply to be seen and heard? Or, equally possible, because they cannot help it, because they are compulsive talkers? Nowadays – and one suspects in the past, too – the taciturn person must be a great rarity in politics. Politicians, with few exceptions, love an audience. Public speaking of one kind or another is as natural to them as breathing and eating. They are not as other men. Some, of course, are better at it than others. Some, talking meaningless rubbish, are more attractive to listen to than others who are doing their not very effective best to produce understandable good sense. What is difficult to accept is the general eulogy of politicians presented by William Safire for American consumption. 'The new, old and constantly changing language of politics', he wrote in the late Sixties,[8] 'is a lexicon of conflict and drama, of ridicule and reproach, of pleading and persuasion. Color and bite permeate a language designed to rally many men, to destroy some, and to change the minds of others.' It is, alas, simply not true that political language, in America or anywhere else, is permeated with colour and bite. Very occasionally one comes across a sentence or, with extreme good fortune, a whole passage which justifies such praise, but for the most part politicians' language is dull stuff, intended to make tarnished ideas or no ideas at all seem bright and glossy, to inflate its author's reputation, to score points off an opponent, or simply to deceive.

'Some political language,' William Safire tells us, 'captures the essence of an abstraction and makes it understandable to millions'. How much, one is entitled to ask, is some? Distressingly few politicians show evidence of this kind of intellectual or verbal ability, although a great many are past-masters of the misleading over-simplification and of the attractive half-truth, which is possibly the reality underneath Safire's pleasant flattery.

Much closer to the reality is Minogue's admirable paragraph on the political virtue of pulling the wool over the eyes, not only of the public or of one's opponents, but of one's colleagues as well.

> 'A good deal of deceit', he observes, 'is essential to the proper working of any kind of institution. Antipathies must be suppressed so that antagonists may work together for various purposes; the extent of support for or opposition to some measure must be falsified, for this knowledge itself will change the situation; and very frequently a politician must disguise his intentions until the time is ripe for revealing them. For timing is often essential to the success or failure of a political move. For these reasons, politicians have elaborated the usages of a

mellifluous and soggy form of discourse, justly famed for its vagueness and ambiguity. The use of this discourse, and the understanding of it, requires enormous skill. Thus in diplomatic communications between powers, the wording of a phrase or the omission of a claim is all that may indicate a major shift in policy. By such devices, political discussion between leaders can go on with the minimum interruption from popular clamour. Political communications must say different things to different people, and preferably can be abandoned or denied if they should cause embarrassment.'[9]

Minogue, it should be noticed, does not approve of politicians' language as such: 'soggy', 'vagueness', and 'ambiguity' are hardly words of praise. But, on the other hand, he seems to accept its inevitability. 'A good deal of deceit is essential', he tells us. 'Antipathies must be suppressed', 'a politician must disguise his intentions', 'political communications must say different things to different people'. The implication is clearly that is we want to be governed at all, we cannot reasonably object to being deceived, since deceit is an essential element of government. 'Popular clamour' has to reduce to the minimum level of nuisance, in order that our rulers can carry out their work on our behalf. 'A good deal of deceit is essential to the proper working of any institution', no matter whether that institution is a government, a university, the General Medical Council or the Marylebone Cricket Club. Experts can work properly only if the public is kept at a comfortable distance and drugged.

It may be so, although such a view suggests that the development of democracy still has some way to go. One is entitled nevertheless to the citizen's privilege of analysing this 'mellifluous and soggy form of discourse, justly famed for its vagueness and ambiguity', and the present book attempts to do precisely this. If one is to be deceived, even in a good cause, it is as well to understand how the process is carried out. Before one begins to assemble the evidence and machinery of deceit, however, two points can usefully be made.

The first is that few of those who are actively and continuously engaged in politics, on either side of the Iron Curtain, understand how stupefyingly boring politics is to the majority of their fellow-citizens. There is a type of human being who needs the excitement, secrecy and power of politics more than he needs food, who spends most of his time, by choice and necessity in the company of similar people and who cannot really understand any other attitude to life. He is that 'political maniac' who regards voting as the highest and most satisfying of a man's activities, far above fatherhood or love, labour for his kin or a good night at the dogs'.[10] I recall a conversation I had some years ago with the wife of a former Cabinet Minister who had lost not only his place in the Cabinet but his seat in Parliament as well, when an election brought about a change of government. He had taken almost immediately to the bottle – heavy drinking is unfortunately a common thing among politicians, as it is among journalists – and only the most devoted efforts of his wife and friends eventually dragged him from the mental and spiritual morass into which he had fallen. Re-election to Parliament effected an almost complete cure. 'Pay no attention,' said his wife, 'to anyone who says there's nothing so dreadful and pitiful as an addiction to drink or drugs, or as the withdrawal symptoms that go with the early stages of a cure. Addiction to politics is infinitely worse. I know. I'm married to a politics addict.'

Most of us, fortunately or unfortunately, are not politics addicts. We find ourselves compelled to involve ourselves in politics to a mild extent at fairly well separated intervals, when we are provided with an opportunity to vote at an election, and some of the doings of politicians may stir us from time to time when we read about them in the newspapers or find them presented to us on television. But day in, day out, we do not find politics absorbing and we are content to leave it to people who do, often with disastrous results. Some of the consequences of this are curious. On television especially, the dedicated politician not infrequently gives the impression of believing that his audience shares his feelings about the importance of politics. Such a person imagines himself to be communicating with millions, whereas in fact he is genuinely communicating with at best thousands and more probably with only hundreds. His political faith and his political in-language, which bind him so closely to his friends, are boring and perplexing to most of his audience, not inspiring and warming.

The second point that should be emphasised at this stage is that modern politicians are not usually humble people. Partly for reasons that will be discussed in the next chapter, they feel compelled to profess their utter rightness and that of their Party, on all possible occasions. Their opponents and critics commit blunders of judgement, weave diabolical plots against humanity and depend on political theories which approach the criminal. They themselves, on the other hand, are enrolled in the Legions of Light and labour unceasingly to show others the path that leads towards the light. They cannot conceivably be wrong and for this reason dogmas can be found liberally scattered throughout their public utterances. In both national and international politics, there is only black and white. The far more interesting, subtle and human shades in between the two extremes cannot be admitted to exist. Poets do not become Congressmen and Congressmen do not write poetry.

The language of politics is not confined to words. Those things which politics think important and unimportant are reflected in the style of the national life. Politics is clothes, eating places, entertainment, literature, films, houses and holidays quite as much as speeches and articles. Sir Harold Wilson's bottle of sauce on the dining table at 10 Downing Street was the language of Labour politics during his tenure of power, his own well-published announcement that he shared the People's Tastes and shunned Elitism. No words could have made the point so well.

A council estate, like an oil-sheikh's Rolls-Royce, is a political statement. These frustratingly small, meanly fitted dwellings in their treeless settings, acres of standardised workers' barracks, announce to the world as plainly as any party manifesto could do: 'We said we would build 200,000 or 400,000 or whatever the figure may have been – dwellings in 1950, 1960, 1970, and by God, we built them. Our political credibility, our power to win working-class votes depended on this. The fact that they are ill-built, poorly furnished, cramped to live in and unimaginatively sited is of no political importance. What matters is that they are all the same – nobody is better off than anyone else – and that we built 200,000, 400,000 of them.' Like the bottle of sauce, they express a political creed, a set of political tactics. They are part of the language of politics, of communication between the rulers and the ruled.

There is nothing particularly or exclusively British about this. As Lionel Brett wrote 30 years ago, in the hopeful, experimental days soon after the end of the Second World War, 'what we call democracy, lacking a unifying mystique, must inevitably lack a unifying style, whether or not the State does most of the building.'[11] Dictatorships use architecture in a bread and circuses manner, to keep the people quiet and to glorify the régime. 'In the struggling social democracies of Western Europe', to use Brett's words, 'architecture is a technique for freeing the whole people from squalor and enabling them to pursue bourgeois ideals in pleasant if unheroic surroundings.'

'The pursuit of bourgeois ideals in pleasant if unheroic surroundings' is an interesting summary and rallying-call of social democracy. Which of its words would today's British, Dutch or Norwegian governments wish to change, and why?

2 Product Differentiation in Politics

A much-favoured technique employed in marketing certain kinds of manufactured goods – detergents and petrol are good examples – is to discover minute, and sometimes imaginary differences between one's own product and those of one's rivals and then to exaggerate and emphasise these differences. This makes Product A distinct, in the public mind, from Product B and, given promotional skill, more desirable. The process is known as product differentiation and it is, to put the matter bluntly, a swindle. Marketing men will say with great conviction, however, that without making use of product differentiation they could hardly sell anything. They would have no tools with which to work. Petrols, instant coffee, cigarettes, washing powders and even cars are so much of a muchness that the public has no logical reason for buying one rather than another. The marketing skill lies in making them seem different.

The marketing managers of the political parties now use much the same approach in order to sharpen the appeal of what they have on offer. It has become known as 'adversary politics' and consists essentially of finding fault with everything one's opponents do and of extolling the virtues of one's own party. If one is a Conservative, all Conservatives are 100 per cent good, intelligent, far-sighted and public-spirited and all Labour people 100 per cent cunning, hypocritical, stupid and blind to the national interest. And all members, without exception, of any trade union or professional organisation one likes to name, from boiler-makers and ring-spinners to doctors and lawyers, are always and naturally highly skilled, hard-working paragons, utterly devoted to the public interest. Against a potentially hostile outside world, the ranks must be firmly closed at all times. It is a somewhat simplistic view. An important part of the case against it 'is that it wastes the time of able politicians in futile parliamentary bickering designed to score points in the battle of the parties, and, indeed, that it discourages many of the most able people from going into politics at all'.[1]

Every issue of *Hansard* nowadays contains examples of product differentiation. Here is one produced in 1972 by a Labour Member, Mr. Arthur Lewis, during the debate on the Finance Bill.

Mr. Arthur Lewis: 'In my constituency, because of the wicked measures introduced by the Government and the savage way in which they have attacked old age pensioners, the sick and the disabled, we have had to introduce meals on wheels.'

Neither Mr. Lewis nor any of his colleagues can really have believed that the members of Mr. Heath's government had been on the rampage against the old and the sick, cutting off their food supplies in a deliberate attempt to starve them to death. The passage quoted is merely a piece of adversary politics. Translated into more reasonable terms, it means that, in Mr. Lewis's opinion, old age pensions and welfare payments have failed to keep pace with inflation and that urgent measures should be taken to improve the situation, the implication being that, had Mr. Lewis's own party been in power, things would have been quite different. Product X nourishes and warms better than Product Y.

The game is played equally assiduously by both sides. In 1968 the Labour Party was in power and on 2nd April the Family Allowances and National Insurance Bill was being debated in the House of Commons. This time it was the turn of a Conservative Member to accuse the Government of conduct which was unseemly in the matter of welfare benefits, with hypocracy thrown in for good measure.

Mr. Eldon Griffiths: 'I want to start with a short quotation from one of my favourite authors on the Government benches. Discussing the social benefits, this very distinguished biographer and historian wrote: "The commitments of the Labour Party's policy, provided that they are not all rushed through in the first year" – which no-one ever suggested – "can be carried out comfortably without any question of increase in the tax burden. On the contrary, they should leave room for substantial tax reductions." This is by my favourite author, the Chancellor of the Exchequer. That is what the Right Hon. gentleman wrote in his elegant and impeccable prose. And some years later he has come

Product Differentiation in Politics 23

to the House and told us of the necessity for some £900 million worth of extra taxation, while asking his Party to support him in cutting sickness, unemployment and injury benefits.'

This is adversary politics in its more elegant House of Commons form. Mr. Griffiths, a good Party man, has been doing his homework. He has discovered a mildly embarrassing statement made by Mr. Jenkins some years earlier which does not match up with a more recent explanation made by the Chancellor in the House. By putting one against the other – an old Parliamentary and journalistic trick – Mr. Griffiths is able to score a fairly easy, but not particularly damaging point. The moral is clear – no Labour Minister can be trusted, no Conservative would behave in such a manner. Product B is less reliable than Product A.

The Trade Unions' marketing policy tends to be carried out with a bludgeon, rather than a rapier. The enemy is to be knocked senseless, rather than teased and tickled with a light weapon and a sharp point. So we have Mr. Briginshaw, of the National Society of Operative Printers, Graphical and Media Personnel, telling the Trades Union Congress[2] that 'the Tories have based their assessment on the view that with the aid of basically repressive class legislation they could push the unions around and get away with it' (i.e. the Conservative Government believed that the Trade Unions should not be a law unto themselves). Product A, the Conservative policy towards trade unions, is always and inevitably 'repressive' and based on 'class'. Product B, the Labour Party policy, always gives the trade unions their just due and knows a good friend when it sees one.

For the trade unionist there is, officially, no such thing as a good employer. The interest of 'the employer' – who is, in more cases than not, a salaried employee – must always be opposed to those of 'the workers'. The trade unions depend for their existence and motivation on what is a carefully fostered piece of folklore, that no common ground is possible between those who give orders and those who take them. The much-treasured phrase 'both sides of industry' must never be allowed to pass out of use. Without an ever-present, implacable enemy, the British trade union movement as we know it would wither away and die. To keep 'both sides of industry' as distinct as possible, every opportunity must be seized and developed to prove that the thoughts, aims and habits of the two are totally dissimilar. So the heads of Civil Service Departments and local authorities, and the boards and departmental managers of the nationalised industries, who have no financial stake in the enterprise whatever, are identified with the 'capitalists' who are exploiting the workers in private industry. They are all lumped together as 'the employers' and they are all, beyond the slightest doubt, 'Tories' at heart, if not actually in fact.

It is mainly for this reason, the need to establish the clearest, sharpest possible product differentiation – a political, not economic need – that the growth of that unmentionable, utterly obscene phenomenon, the self-employed manual worker, had to be dropped with all speed and ruthlessness. The self-employed bricklayer or plasterer bridged the essential, God-given gap between the 'employers' and the 'workers'. If such a situation were allowed to continue, the unions' well-understood and highly profitable marketing policy would disintegrate. Product A would become indistinguishable from Product B.

So the heaviest verbal guns were brought into action. The increasingly popular habit of hiring self-employed labour had to be blown into a million pieces, not methodically argued away.

'The practice has grown,' W. E. Winterbottom, of the Draughtsmen's and Allied Technicians' Association, told Congress in 1967, 'because it enables employers to avoid their legal and industrial obligations. It is costly and it is inefficient. But employers can dodge national insurance contributions, industrial training levy, selective employment tax, their obligations under the Contracts of Employment Act, and redundancy payments. They do not have to pay for holidays and they do not have to pay for absence due to sickness. But, much more important from our point of view, they can dodge nationally negotiated conditions of employment and can avoid their obligations to meet and negotiate with the trade unions under agreed procedures. The employer who would otherwise need to improve conditions to attract labour can run down his own labour force and make up the numbers with the ready-to-hand blackleg force on his premises.'[3]

This passage contains a remarkable number of false statements and distortions. From the employer's point of view, it is neither 'costly' nor 'inefficient' to use self-employed labour. On the contrary, because men can be hired as and when required and only in the numbers needed at any particular time, it is a very efficient way of using labour, especially since, as Mr. Winterbottom himself points out, the only payment made is for work done. The vast burden of social contributions does not have to be shouldered at all. It is true that a price has to be paid for this. The self-employed man has to demand and receive more per hour than the employed man, precisely because he has no cushion of social security to fall back on. But, even allowing for this, the net cost to the employer of an hour's work performed by a self-employed person is considerably lower than it is for someone employed in the traditional way. The use of self-employed labour may be politically unwise or even immoral. It may be strongly disliked by the Inland Revenue, which finds it convenient and reliable to have tax deducted at source by the employer. But to say that it is 'costly and inefficient' is simply a lie. By using words like these, together with such loaded expressions as 'dodge national insurance contributions', 'avoid their obligations to meet and negotiate with the trade unions', and 'the ready-to-hand blackleg force on his premises', Mr. Winterbottom is indulging in polemic and abuse, not reasoned argument. The Goodies are trade union wage earners, the Baddies are the self-employed, and their respective outlines must be kept sharp and clear. This is product differentiation at its most obvious.

But, in order to make the difference between Product A and Product B clear to even the meanest intelligence, the Bad Workingman has to be planted firmly in the pillory and every available squashed tomato and rotten egg thrown at him. Like the Bad Employer, he must be persuaded to abandon his evil ways. He has yielded to temptation and he must repent. Mr. Winterbottom, who is clearly a practised hand at the business of dealing firmly with sinners, has a large supply of verbal eggs and tomatoes in his basket. Here he is, warming to his task and sparing nothing.

> The attraction to workers lies in the opportunity for tax-dodging. A draughtsman on this racket can get tax relief for many things for which the ordinary worker can get no relief. For example, he gets relief on the cost of the fares to work. Because this is a cost entailed in his one-man business, he can get relief on the purchase of a car, because this is bought for use in his business; he can get relief on the cost of his domestic telephone for his business. He gets it on meals and even the housekeeping money paid to his wife becomes a wage paid to her as his secretary in his one-man business. Mortgage payments on his house are relieved of tax because he has registered his house as his business premises.

And at this point Mr. Winterbottom, in his role as God's agent, poises himself for the kill. Solid, innocent working men are being tempted by the Devil, with tax-relief as the bait on his fiendish hook. 'Those who operate these agencies make no contribution to the economy nor to society. They are purveyors of bodies. Indeed, it might well be said that the practice ought to be covered by the Street Offences Act. It represents a new and vicious form of prostitution.'

Having decided that society must, for its own good and eventual salvation, be kept in a state of perpetual warfare between two irreconcilable opposites until one or the other is totally defeated, truly professional politicians, inside and outside an elected assembly, will instinctively reject any overtures of peace from the other side, any suggestions of compromise or common ground. There must be no parleying with the enemy, no acknowledgement of the possibility that there might be some good ideas and some good people on both sides. Product A is a useless menace and no decent shop should stock it; Product B is a wonder-working benefit to mankind, a miracle cure, no home should be without it. Any hint that both A and B are a waste of money and that what the customers are really longing for is Product C, which is not yet on the market, has to be ruthlessly squashed. War is war and it can only be waged in strictly black and white terms, or so the activists believe.

An interesting illustration of this fight-on-till-the-enemy-lies-flat-at-our-feet approach appeared in a recent issue of the left-wing youth publication, *Challenge*.[4] The heading of the article was 'Edward Heath Rejects Class War for the Denim Revolution'. It had been sparked off by a remark made by Mr. Heath at the Conservative Party Conference, to the effect that jeans were helping to break down class-barriers between young people. This was an attempt to de-polarise politics, to persuade the lamb and the lion to sit down peacefully together, that *Challenge* simply could not allow. Class-war and the revolution had to go on. Left was Left and Right was Right, permanently and unalterably.

So we had this, in the no-literary-nonsense style that *Challenge* had adopted as a proof of its democratic instincts and classlessness:

> Old Ted praised jeans for breaking down class barriers amongst our generation – so he reckons we're all one class, all in the same boat, does he? Well, I've got news for Mr. Heath and his upper class cronies – class barriers and differences do still exist

among us kids. Alright the differences may be more subtle than twenty years ago but they are still there.

Just'cos some well-to-do public schoolboy puts a pair of Levi's on in his spare time (when he's not doing his 'prep' chaps) that doesn't mean there's no class difference between him and the rest of us.

The lesson is then rammed home. Upper-class children – never defined on these occasions, but meaning, for political purposes, not working-class, the enemy, the bosses, the employers – go to schools which 'can buy the best teachers and facilities'; 'most kids' go to comprehensives, which have no money for books or equipment, and where the teachers are inferior, all the best teachers having been creamed off by the public schools, 'because they pay them more'. Public schoolboys go to the university, working-class children have to go straight to work. But, anyway, there isn't any work. The children of the upper classes get good jobs on the old-boy network; for the rest it's the dole or the dead-end job.

'So,' says the author of the article, 'I'll say this to you Mr. Heath [the omission of the commas is deliberate; it makes the writing more democratic. Punctuation is an 'upper-class' affair, one of the enemy's weapons] you're either really naive or your [accurate spelling is upper-class, too] trying to take us kids for a ride – 'cos classes amongst youth do exist and just 'cos we all wear jeans it doesn't alter the fact.' And, anyway, because of capitalist greed and exploitation, the price of jeans is so high that 'I wonder if many of us can afford to buy a decent pair anyway'.

It is a text-book example of product differentiation. Product A smells sweeter, tastes better, contains more food value, can be guaranteed not to poison you and, above all, is made by an honest firm. Under no circumstances can it be confused with that utterly spurious, dangerous article, Product B, at least by a shopper who, thanks to the consumer advice provided by *Challenge*, keeps his wits about him.

The effect, and intention, are curiously similar to that of the medieval morality plays. On the one hand, the forces of good and on the other the forces of evil. All that is required for success is to keep the appearance and characteristics of the two unmistakably different and separate, no matter what degree of exaggeration and misrepresentation has to be used in the process. Subject only to the law of libel, politicians have an encouragingly free hand in the matter, far beyond what is allowed to commercial advertisers. If the British Trades Descriptions Act and Advertising Code were to be applied to political marketing, many politicians, at all levels, would find their style considerably cramped.

Political marketing skills really come to the surface at election time. It is at this moment that Product A has got to be shown to be beyond all possible doubt superior to Product B. Nowadays, the election product is mainly the party programme and the party leadership, for which the local candidate is little more than an agent, the Leader's approved representative in the provinces. As an agent, he is required to have a reasonable credibility and attractiveness of his own, however. This often produces considerable marketing problems, since the candidate has to be presented as a solid, typical citizen and as a good party man, yet with qualities his opponent lacks. Since very much the same person is attracted to a political life, no matter what his party label may be, product differentiation is a tricky business. Teachers, lecturers, lawyers, with a few businessmen, doctors and accountants, make up the stable mix nowadays, with no significant difference between the personal background and life-style of the representatives of one party and another. But, since politics demands a difference, a difference there has to be. Mr. Wedgwood Benn and Mrs. Shirley Williams may be as Oxbridge and middle-class as they come, but, if Mrs. Williams' hair is cunningly untidy and if both of them have children at comprehensive schools, they can be marketed as decent, ordinary, average people, totally different from the class-bound Conservative who fritter their wealth away on hairdressing and clothes and send their sons and daughters to élitist boarding schools.

Until recently, the candidates at British General Elections were colour-coded, so that the public could always tell them apart – blue for Conservative, red for Labour, orange for Liberal. The candidates and their more active supporters wore rosettes of the appropriate colour and posters and campaign literature reinforced the colour-message. So far as voters were concerned, it was a kindly and considerate act; however confused one might be after reading the candidate's biography, the colour kept one's eye on the right target. Jones (Labour), Smith (Conservative) and Robinson (Liberal) might all be teachers or barristers or accountants but, so long as Smith was blue one could never go wrong. The same helpful principle used to be followed at municipal elections, but during the past five years, at both local and national elections, there has been considerable backsliding, partly, no doubt, because we live in hard times and colour printing is more expensive than black and white.

The managerial problem in politics is to know whether one is trying to market a real person or a puppet. It is very difficult to do both at once, since the candidate has to be put on show and people have to meet him, even if his main function is to function as the party programme on two legs. The usual way of trying to overcome the difficulty is to put the real person, or a suitably cosmetic version of him, on the outside of the leaflet and the party programme inside, together with a summary of the great services the candidate has rendered to the constituency since the last election. What happens in Bristol is typical of the country as a whole.

Here, for instance, is the back page biography of Arthur Palmer, the Labour Member for Bristol North-East, set out for the benefit of the electors in October 1974.

> Arthur Palmer has had considerable experience of public and parliamentary life. After a period as a Town Councillor he first entered the House of Commons at the age of 32. A chartered engineer, he is active in all matters affecting industry, science and technology. He is chairman of the Select Committee on Science and Technology. Arthur Palmer takes a keen interest in all Bristol affairs, including social welfare, education, aviation, transport, docks and housing. He is an active trade unionist.

Inside, on page 2 of the folder, we have the Goodies and Baddies line-up, the virtuous record of the Labour Government and the shameful, near-criminal behaviour of the Conservative opposition, with no direction whatever with what Mr. Palmer himself may have done, although an unconvincing and unnecessary attempt is made to pull him into the manifesto by means of such phrases as 'I will say this', and 'Our opponents, Conservatives and Liberals alike'. It is, in fact, a testimonial to which the candidate puts his hand and seal, a public tribute to the party leadership repeated in one constituency after another all over the country.

> For seven months the Labour Government has had to carry all the responsibilities of office without a parliamentary majority behind it. Bearing in mind the difficulties they have faced, Labour Ministers have achieved great things; if anyone doubts that statement let him or her recall the grim position of our

country last February: A partial blackout, unemployment and a 3-day working week; due to the obstinacy of Mr. Heath and mismanagement by the Conservatives of their relations with the trade unions. Today there are still serious problems to be solved, notably inflation, but there is a healthier climate of hope and opportunity all round. Instead of confrontation, the Labour Government has inaugurated co-operation and a working partnership with the trade unions. Let no one be deceived. Modern industrial societies can't be governed against the unions; the Tories made the attempt and led us nearly to disaster. They must not be allowed to put the country at risk again.

In other fields the Labour Government has achieved many successes in a short time. It has stemmed the rise in living costs both for owner-occupiers and tenants. The elderly and disabled have been awarded the largest rise ever in pensions. Food costs have been contained by sensible subsidies. In a time of stringency the better-off have been asked to contribute the most and the property speculator held in check for the first time. I have set out on this page a brief summary of Labour's proposals for the future. These are practical, progressive and related to the country's needs. Our opponents – Conservatives and Liberals alike – have no policies that show any kind of consistency. That is why they spend so much time attacking us and trying to scare people about nationalisation. On that topic, in any case there is a doubt remaining in a single person's mind, I will say this: We shall use nationalisation as a convenient tool in situations where private industry cannot or will not do the job. And where large sums of taxpayers' money are being pumped into private firms we shall insist on public participation and social responsibility. The Labour Party accepts a mixed economy: part public, part private, each sector contributing to the health of the whole and deserving adequate incentives.'

Pictures of wives and often family groups are included in these appeals to the electorate, in the hope and belief that they will show the candidate to be a normal human being, even though he is a politician, and certainly not a homosexual, just in case there should happen to be any fears on that score. Sometimes the wife is pressed into service to contribute a little signed piece of her own, usually to the effect that we all have problems nowadays in paying our bills, don't we, and prices are bound to go up if the Conservatives, or whichever party is case as the no-good Product B, gets into power. This is supposed to help to capture the Woman's Vote.

The Conservatives proceed in exactly the same way. This is another of the Bristol Members, Robert Cooke, packaged for the same 1974 General Election. First, a few personal details:

> Robert Cooke, born 1930 (MP for Bristol West since March 1957), is married to Jennifer, daughter of Evelyn King, MP. Patric Cooke is 7 and Louise 3.
> In the complex world in which we now live Mr. Cooke has found in seventeen years in the Commons that the Member of Parliament is, all too often, the last remaining defence against the power of the State. Although a loyal and senior member of a Party at Westminster, Mr. Cooke has never been afraid to take an independent line when occasion demands.
> He is the author of "Government and the Quality of Life", just published, in which he outlines some original ideas for improving the Environment, and for the Arts and Broadcasting.

Then a piece of conventional fury against Labour – always called Socialist – misdeeds and mismanagement:

> It is a sad fact that every Socialist Government in our history has greatly increased taxation and at the same time run the nation heavily into debt. Taxes are now proposed which are aimed not at rising revenue for necessary public expenditure, but have as their sole purpose the destruction of private property. Do not imagine for a moment that a Socialist Wealth Tax would long remain above the heads of most of us. There is no incentive to save under socialism thus they add further to inflation. Conservative governments have always, over a parliament, reduced taxes and encouraged savings and investment.'

It is impossible to know whether this kind of heroes and villains performance achieves anything useful or not. The electors expect it, but who knows how many of them are influenced by the literature or indeed read it. There is good evidence to believe that most of them have made up their minds long before the election campaign begins – this phenomenon is discussed in the next chapter – and that the posturing and sword-waving which characterise elections are found by many people to be either tedious or funny. The candidates themselves are extremely unlikely to see anything humorous in the situation. Politics and a sense of humour very rarely go together.

It is possible that Americans are different. The principal of a successful public relations firm in California, Clem Whitaker, is on record as saying that there are only two ways in which the average American can be persuaded to take an interest in an election campaign.

> Most every American loves contest. He likes a good hot battle, with no punches pulled. He likes the clash of arms! So *you can interest him if you put on a fight*!
>
> No matter what you fight for, *fight for something*, in our business, and very soon the voters will be turning out to hear you, providing you make the fight interesting.
>
> Then, too, most every American likes to be entertained. He likes the movies; he likes mysteries; he likes fireworks and parades. He likes Jack Benny and Bob Hope and Joe E. Brown!
>
> So, if you can't fight, PUT ON A SHOW! And if you put on a good show, Mr. and Mrs. America will turn out to see it.[5]

These inspiring words were spoken thirty years ago, as part of an address to the Los Angeles Chapter of the Public Relations Society of America in 1948. There is no reason to suppose that the situation today is any different, except that television has appeared, as a competitor for the show and fight business. So is Whitaker's analysis correct? Can the public become interested in politics only if it is presented to them in terms of one armed champion attacking another? Must a discussion, an exchange of views, an explanation, become a violent brawl before more than a handful of people can be persuaded to pay any attention to the subject or to the people involved? Is adversary politics, based as it is on antagonism, rather than on a wish to arrive at an understanding, based on a shrewd assessment of the public mind?

Many experienced observers would say yes, and they would include a majority of those who earn a living by arranging political discussions and interviews on television. The more heat and fury the occasion produces, the more successful it is reckoned to have been as a piece of television, and the higher the skill of the chairman or interviewer is rated. For all their denials, made as a matter of routine, television producers and directors are all in favour of adversary politics. They are all in favour of screen-battles and they do everything they can to bring them about. If a discussion between two politicians belonging to opposing parties reveals a substantial measure of agreement between them and if the tone remains quiet, even and civilised throughout, something has clearly gone. Either the wrong people have been invited to take part of there has been a failure of professional expertise.

The Liberal, the man in the middle, is liable to be an embarrassment on these occasions and, in private, most television producers would admit to wishing that he did not exist. He is liable to take the edge off the fight, to soften the longed-for clash between Left and Right. The problem is partly physical. In the threesome discussions that British television is wont to organise at election times, and occasionally for ad hoc purposes as well, the inclination to put the Labour spokesman at one end of a table and the Conservative at the other, with the Liberal, who is written off as neither fish nor fowl nor good red herring, in the middle, where he symbolises nothing but his middleness, is strong. Given only two speakers, one Right and one Left, they can be put at two separate tables, glaring at one another like two fighting cocks.

Some politicians have made clear their objections to being cast in the role of fighting cocks. Politics, they say, is a serious business and to convert it into a form of sport for the entertainment industry is to debase it and to impoverish society. In Britain, Mr. Wedgwood Benn and the late Richard Crossman have given strong support to this view, accusing television of trivialising politics and of showing too much interest in elections, its most combative aspect. Those who see the situation in this way criticise especially the instinct which they say television producers have for seeing politics as a dramatic struggle and of turning what are essentially conflicts of ideas into conflicts of personalities. The plan is to give viewers a ringside seat at a political prize-fight.

The argument does not completely hold water. To begin with, it is certainly not true, as Mr. Crossman and Mr. Benn have suggested, that in one camp one finds all the politicians, serious-minded, philosophical fellows, wholly concerned with the public good, and in the other all the showmen, sensationalists and political impresarios. The implication is that, if it were not for the evil, corrupting influence of television, the public would drop its obsession with political quarrels and personalities and 'crises' and discover an interest in political theory and organisation. The notion is both false and hypocritical, false because, as we have already said, a passionate, life-long interest in politics is reserved for a special kind of mind and temperament, and hypocritical, because the politicians themselves, completely outside the framework of television, indulge heavily in the habit of personalising and dramatising political activity and debate. Television does no more than continue and possibly intensify what the politicians are already doing, apparently with gusto. One can deplore adversary politics, but television did not create it. It is certain that many politicians produce a far from agreeable impression on the television screen, but that is not necessarily the fault of television, any more than a mirror is the cause of an ugly woman's ugliness. Television is too often used as a whipping boy by politicians who cannot bring themselves to believe that either they or their ideals are, for most people, dull and boring. When they accuse a television producer or interviewer of trying to 'dramatise' a situation, all the unfortunate man may be trying to do is to make the best of a bad job, of squeezing as much interest from the subject as he can. That, after all, is what he is paid to do.

As studies carried out in both America and Britain have shown, television, sober or sensational, does practically nothing to change people's political allegiances. Viewers may like to see politicians on the screen occasionally, as part of the human panorama and possibly for their entertainment value, but the effect on their political opinions is practically nil.[6] Their opinion of politicians is not necessarily the same as their political opinions, of course, and, in the public mind, politicians may well emerge from television worse than they went in.

It is as right and proper that politicians should be immersed in political theory as that clergymen should be immersed in theology, so long as being immersed is not confused with drowning. It is right, too, that politicians should have principles and that we should know what they are, especially those which motivate the particular politician who has been elected to represent us. But this does not necessarily mean that such principles would make absorbing material for a television programme, assuming, that is, that they were to be presented as principles, straight, unadorned and in no way dramatised. Here, for example, are the first six on Mr. Benn's list of 'the simple socialist principles that inspire the Labour Movement', set out in his election address of October 1974.

X We must have the right to decide whether we want Britain in the Common Market and be free to vote to come out.

- **X** We must have the right to own or control our huge new oil reserves discovered round our shores.
- **X** We must insist that the whole community owns the urban land we require for homes, schools and hospitals where possible.
- **X** We must see today that the huge monopolies which dominate British Industry and keep prices high are made accountable to the National (sic) and to their own employees.
- **X** We must have a much fairer tax system, and get away from the injustice of the rating system, too.
- **X** We must end the inequalities that still divide our people into two nations from birth, through school and working life, on to retirement.

Without in any way objecting to or criticising these principles as such, one might be permitted to feel that they would need a little professional treatment before the average viewer would find them compelling television material. Illustration, discussion, disagreement – some trick of the impresario would be required to bring them sufficiently alive to justify screen-time.

The television producer's and reporter's dilemma and despair with regard to politics was admirably expressed by Richard West ten years ago. 'Those of us,' he said, 'who have had to sit through a party conference may well consider why T.V. should be interested. The debate is of low quality: the proceedings are generally arranged to the benefit of the platform; the real excitement and quarrelling are confined to private meetings in hotel rooms.'[7] Where, of course, the cameras and microphones cannot go. If they could, there is no doubt that viewers would find the results absorbing. No dramatisation would be required. The jealousies, the scheming, the decisions on tactics, the obvious antagonisms would provide everything a producer could desire. And this, it might be pointed out, is one of the major reasons why politicians find politics so interesting and why the public, and television producers, usually find it so tedious. The politicians are taking part in the behind-the-scenes stuff in the hotel bedrooms, the offices and the private houses; the ordinary citizen is supposed to be not only satisfied, but exhilarated by the version of events which the party managers consider safe for public consumption. It is a lot to ask.

At this point one can usefully ask for whom product discrimination and adversary politics are really intended. Are such techniques mainly to help the public to get its bearings, to avoid having to confess, 'I really don't know whom to vote for. They all seem the same to me.'? Do they, as commercial advertising is supposed to do, perform the indispensable function of making the machine work? Or is their purpose similar to that of religious exercises for the faithful, strengthening the will and keeping the head turned in the right direction? When a Labour Member of Parliament engages in nit-picking at the expense of the Conservatives, is he doing this primarily to demonstrate to his colleagues in the Party that he has the full repertoire of political tricks at his command, to infuriate his opponents, or simply to make himself feel good?

What seems certain is that, with whole populations conditioned by the constant publicity given to competitive sport and by journalistic and commercial superlatives and gross oversimplification, politicians are unlikely to attract much attention unless they adopt similar methods at least for some of the time. Something of the order of 'Conservatives Rule' daubed and scrawled on walls all over Britain seems indicated, if an interest in politics is to extend beyond a very small minority.

Richard West's comment on the private excitement and the public dullness of politics has already been quoted. He goes on to state his belief that things are dealt with better in the United States, where 'politics make rich and exciting T.V.'. The Americans, however, have certain important advantages which are denied to the British.

'The most exciting political T.V. spectacles,' he feels, 'are the conventions where the two big parties meet to choose their Presidential candidates. The interest lies in the fight for power and not in any argument over principles. English viewers experienced the same excitement in 1963, when the Tories wrangled over a choice of leader, and even in 1960, when Hugh Gaitskell was fighting for his political life. But these were exceptional cases.'

It is not easy to see why drama in political life should be regarded as a bad thing or why the public should be blamed for wanting it and welcoming it. It is essential, however, to make a distinction between real drama and bogus, contrived drama. The televised hearings on Vietnam or on the Watergate affair in the United States Senate were real drama. They went on for days on end, and some witnesses faced the Senators for hours. The questioning and argument were ruthless, detailed and, beyond doubt, intellectually stimulating.

Senator Baker   Mr. Barker, you are 55 years old.
Mr. Barker   Fifty-six.
Senator Baker   You have a real estate business in Miami; you were previously involved in the Bay of Pigs operations for the CIA. You are a veteran of the U.S. Army in World War II where you were a captain the Army Air Corps, and you were a German prisoner of war for 17 months.
Mr. Barker   Sixteen months.
Senator Baker   Mr. Barker, what on earth would motivate you at your station in life, at your age, and with that background, to do something that surely you knew to be illegal?
Mr. Barker   Senator, E. Howard Hunt, under the name of Edwardo, represents to the Cuban people their liberation. I cannot deny my services in the way that it was proposed to me on a matter of national security, knowing that, with my training, I had personnel available for this type of operation. I could not deny this request at the time.
Senator Baker   Why?
Mr. Barker   Because I felt it was my duty to comply with Mr. Hunt's request.
Senator Baker   Why?
Mr. Barker   Because it involved a matter of national security.
Senator Baker   Why?
Mr. Barker   Because this was a service to my country, sir.
Senator Baker   What national security?
Mr. Barker   Discovering information about a person who I had been told by Mr. Hunt was a traitor, who was passing – he or his associates – to a foreign embassy.
Senator Baker   Who?
Mr. Barker   Pardon me. (Conferring with Counsel.) The Soviet Embassy.
Senator Baker   Who?
Mr. Barker   Who? I do not understand. Who what, sir?
Senator Baker   Who was passing the information to the Soviet Embassy?
Mr. Barker   At that time Mr. Ellsberg's name was not mentioned. Mr. Ellsberg's name was mentioned to me a half hour

before the surreptitious entry; then when I found out the name of the person involved –
Senator Baker   What was the connection between the allegations of the Ellsberg situation and the imminent and impending break-in into the Democratic National Committee headquarters at the Watergate complex?
Mr. Barker   At that time, none. After that Ellsberg, we came up on a matter involving security. At the death of Mr. Hoover, the third time –
Senator Baker   At the request of Mr. Hoover?
Mr. Barker   At the death of Mr. Hoover.
Senator Baker   At the what?
Mr. Barker   At the death of Mr. Hoover.
Senator Baker   At the death of Mr. Hoover. Why did you come up then?
Mr. Barker   I came up with about 10 Cubans to infiltrate this group for security reasons.
Senator Baker   What group?'[8]

This is genuine political drama. One does not even have to see the Senate hearings on televisions to be caught up in excitement. The published transcript of them has all the excitement and tension of a first-class novel. One cannot put it down. The contrast with the House of Commons tomfoolery quoted above is sadly marked.

To accuse the Conservatives of making 'savage attacks' on old people and invalids is bogus drama. Such methods can easily backfire. One of the reasons why so many people, in all countries, have turned their backs on politics is because they have become disgusted with the methods of politicians. After a while, the tactics of blaming all the national misfortunes on the other side cease to work and those who practise them are written off as a troupe of mountebanks, unworthy of serious attention.

3 Getting and Holding Power

Men, and to a much lesser extent women, are prepared to go to extraordinary lengths to get political power. They will invest substantial sums of their own money in campaigning, sacrifice health, comfort and domestic peace, put up with almost unlimited amounts of public criticism and abuse, and risk the humiliation and disappointment of defeat. The phenomenon is international and quite independent of political systems. Why do they do it?

The answer is bound to be complicated. Any individual may have several reasons for deciding to embark on a political career, some reputable and worth publicising, some essentially very private. Here one can only suggest possibilities, based partly on observable facts, partly on the admissions of politicians themselves, and partly on conversations with one's friends. There may be a tradition of politics in the family, with one generation after another providing Members of Parliament, Congressmen or Senators. A man may take unusual pleasure in the sound of his own voice, needing plenty of opportunity to make speeches as other people require sport or women. The salary and pension available to members of the legislature may appear not unattractive. Status in the community, the pleasure of possessing secret information, the opportunities for travel at the public expense may all play a part. The wish to be useful, to perform some kind of public service, is not to be discounted; the observer of politics should not fall into the trap of becoming a hundred per cent cynical.

But at the centre of the wish to enter politics, whether at the local or the national level, there usually seems to be a strong urge for something which is best called power, although the term is not a satisfactory one. Power, in this sense, includes not only the ability to influence the course of events and to control other people's actions but also the feeling of being at the centre of things, the place where decisions are made and where important discussions take place. The satisfactions provided by 'power' are relative, because power itself is relative. An opposition back-bench Member of Parliament has far less 'power' than the Prime Minister or the people who compose his Cabinet, but he has far more of it than the majority of the men and women who elected him. A local councillor has no national power at all, but he may well have considerable say in the matter of public expenditure and public appointments. An autocratic ruler has a degree of power over his subjects, power to imprison them, deprive them of a livelihood or even kill them, which is denied to the President of the United States. Yet the President would certainly and rightly consider himself to be a very powerful political power. The essence of the satisfaction which power brings is not so much any measure or definition of that power as the morale-raising knowledge that other people have not got it. It is this, the yearning to be more powerful than one's fellow-citizens and in this way to stand a better chance of imposing one's ideas on others which constitutes the central appeal of any kind of power, and certainly of political power.

And, of course, power is a staircase, or can be. If he is ambitious – he usually is, at least in the early stages of his career – the politician will want to move steadily up the stairs, acquiring a little more power at each tread. He will fight very hard indeed to make this kind of progress, accepting all the constraints on behaviour and inclination which the party managers demand of him. He will, to use an elegant phrase, be extremely careful to keep his nose clean at all times.

Some politicians, but not many, are not ambitious at all, being well content to be where they are. I remember, in the mid-Fifties, being in the Smoking Room of the House of Commons with a bright Junior Minister with whom I had just had lunch. He pointed out a group of four or five elderly Members – all Labour Members – sitting peacefully in a corner, chatting, dozing and smoking their pipes. 'We all know', he said, 'that the House of Commons has been described by generations as the best club in the country. Well, that's what it means. They'd be heartbroken if they were to lose their membership of it and that's why winning an election's so vital to them. They never give any trouble and you can always depend on them.' This may, perhaps, seem to be rather low-key political power but it is important to those who have it, a comment which might be made of any kind of power, at any level.

In studying what politicians say and do, it is wise to know quite a lot about them as people, in order to be in a position to assess how much the job matters to the man one is observing at the moment. A politician's public language is a screen, a false scent, a safety net – the range of possible metaphors is a wide one – quite as much as it is a form of expression. Given the prime necessity that he and his party shall not lose power or office, almost everything he says and writes is calculated to make that dreadful possibility less likely. And, even for those quite a long way from the very top, there can be a great deal to lose. In the United States, an important Senator can have a personal staff of 150 people. Even a much less powerful and senior Senator can be provided with as many as 50 people to assist and serve him. They will carry out many of the duties which a British member of the House of Commons or House of Lords is accustomed to perform for himself with the help of a single secretary, such as reading through letters from constituents. The Senator's staff will write memos on this correspondence, to 'sensitise' him to problems. It would be difficult for the person at the centre of such a court not to feel important, even by American standards. But even the Senator's European counterparts, with their somewhat more modest style of official living, would feel that they had a great deal to lose.

In such circumstances the motto 'Office before Honour' – the phrase is Mr. Enoch Powell's[1] – is likely to have a strong appeal. Given a straight choice between power and principle, says Mr. Powell, the modern politician will prefer power every time. His former colleagues in the Conservative Party, he observed, 'knew quite well that they were going back on the essentials of what the party stood for. Many of them, faintly to their credit, were ashamed of themselves and loathed the draught the Prime Minister was forcing them to swallow. But if they did not exactly 'relax and enjoy it', they submitted. Between 1972 and 1974 the Prime Minister 'forced them to abandon every promise and principle on which they had been elected'.

It is somewhat unusual for a politician to accuse his own Party of breaking its election promises and throwing its avowed principles overboard. That privilege is usually reserved for one's political opponents. But Mr. Powell is by no means the usual kind of modern politician. He does, it appears, value principle more than office, and he resigns when the Government he was elected to support fails, in his opinion, to honour its promises. Resignations are extremely rare among politicians nowadays. They go only when, for one reason or another, they are compelled to. President Nixon's desperate efforts to hold on to office illustrate the point on the grand scale. Mr. Powell, however, has indicated a fundamental problem which has to be faced by anyone who is active in political life. Make no promises, and few people will vote for either you or your party. Make promises and state principles, and circumstances will compel you to go back on them. Go back on them and you will let the enemy in, unless you are able to think up some exceedingly skilful double-talk which will convince the electors, or enough of them, that what you originally said did not mean what your critics say it meant.

Principles and promises are indeed a politician's nightmare. He would wish them away gladly and with much relief, but he cannot do without them. They are his albatross, hanging for ever around his neck and bring ultimate doom to his ship. Looking back a few years, the Conservative party will shudder to remember what it said in 1972:

> 'We and only WE will slow down the desperate rise in prises'
> 'We will once again create the incentives for new enterprises; this is the only way to create new jobs'
> 'We will eliminate the causes of the reduction in house building'
> 'We will concentrate on providing homes for the elderly'
> 'A Conservative Government will provide incentives to stop people wanting to emigrate'
> 'We will, as a first priority, do for Pensioners the one really essential thing: control the cost of living'
> 'We will re-introduce parental choice in education'
> 'We will do something about bringing Trade Union Law up-to-date. Our plans are well prepared and simple. Bring Trade Unions within the law – a law not amended since 1906.'

and so on. 'Will', it might be remarked, is a strong word; it is not the same as 'try', which is a wiser and more modest word, but not, apparently, considered strong enough to win elections. 'Will' is, however, much more likely to be used by the Party which was not in office at the time of the Election. It has to rely on some form of future tense, because it has no very recent achievements of its own to offer. The Party which has just left office and is hoping to take it up again is likely to appeal to the electorate in this fashion, looking happily, if selectively, backward and pointing, wherever possible, to the vastly inferior achievements of its opponents at the same time.

LABOUR'S ACHIEVEMENTS

The Labour Government has done what needed to be done. It

has put first things first – pensions, for example; it has not feared unpopularity – unpopularity fomented and exaggerated by the hate campaigns of the Tory press. Its RECORD OF ACHIEVEMENT is now recognised abroad and by fair-minded observers at home.

THE ECONOMY – A Strong Britain
Our balance of payments situation is better than at any time since 1945. The surplus for the year ending last March was over £550 million (the target had been £300 million). Roy Jenkins has been an honest and realistic Chancellor. He was not prepared to bring in an electioneering budget, as the Tories used to do. The pound is strong, exports high, and our international debts have been halved.'

and

HOUSING – More Homes than Ever
For many of us this is the most urgent of all problems. The Tories talk of broken promises. But our record speaks for itself.
  1,550,000 houses completed under the Tories (1959–64)
  1,961,000 houses completed under Labour (1964–69)
Labour's Rent Act freed tenants from the fear of eviction. Exorbitant rents can now be prevented; independent tribunals operate to decide fair rents. We have eased the burden of rates by generous grants to local authorities and rebates for those in need; pensioners and low-wage earners have greatly benefited Labour has increased home improvement grants, preserving much-needed housing. Tories plan to slash housing subsidies and abolish rent controls.

This approach might be described as attempting to gain or regain power by means of the partisan presentation of factual information. But what evidence is there that many people are in fact influenced one way or another by such tactics? Is the main value and perhaps purpose of these catalogues of achievements to confirm the faithful in their faith, rather than to tip the waverers the right way over the edge or to convert those of another creed? What does determine voting habits, the head or the heart? In the last resort, surely, one gives one's vote to the candidate or the party with whom one can most easily identify oneself. 'This,' one says, 'is where I belong. This is where I find my sort of people.'

The successful candidate, or party, is successful, therefore, because he or it symbolises what a majority of voters think of as themselves and their way of life. Politicians, especially in Britain, are very unwilling to admit this. They find it more flattering to believe and to say that the decision to vote for this candidate or that represents an entirely rational choice, based on a careful and intelligent appraisal of the facts. The Americans are a good deal more realistic, at least in public. The belief in the folk hero lingers on strongly in the United States, where it is possible for a book like Lloyd Warner's *The Living and the Dead: a Study of the Symbolic Life of Americans*[2] to be taken perfectly seriously. The 'study', which is cast in fictional form, is built around the central character of Biggy Muldoon, 'a political hero', who rises from rags to riches to become Mayor of Yankee City. He succeeds politically because he is a folk hero, who 'expresses fundamental and important themes of the culture in which he is found'.

Such a hero, it appears, is of vital importance, both for society and for the individuals who are attracted by him. He functions in three ways. 'His actual presence stimulates those who believe in him to project their own private feelings and beliefs directly on him. His presence also serves as a model for their imitation and learning and for the measurement of their own moral inadequacies. Further, the hero arouses the hopes and fears of those who believe in him, and he energizes and gives social direction to some of their anxieties.' He is 'the champion of the people, the strong man who attacks the proud and powerful and protects the poor and lowly.'

There has not been a British folk hero quite like this for a considerable time. British politicians, especially those at the top, take great pains to present what they conceive to be the image of the most trusted, least suspect figure in the national life, solid; sport-loving; sharp and intelligent but in no way intellectual, friendly, approachable; and, ideally, with an accent that belongs to no particular social class. The British like their Prime Ministers in particular to have an avuncular flavour about them. Baldwin, Churchill, Wilson, Heath and Callaghan have fitted the bill very well. They have aroused the sympathies of the public quite as much by their appearance as by anything they have said. The language with which they have gained power has been physical, a matter of looks, quite as much as verbal. At the time when it mattered, a majority of the electorate has considered them trustworthy, of the right type to carry out the job. Once the majority of the electorate ceases to identify themselves with him, the Prime Minister, like the President, is lost.

It goes without saying that the higher the office, the more skilfully a man will have to campaign to get it and the harder, and possibly more unscrupulously his opponents will have to work to prevent him. No politics are entirely clean, but some are dirtier than others, and the dirtiest tactics are to be expected as one nears the top. The campaign for the Presidency of the United States attracts an above-average share of mud-slinging and character-assassination. The same has been true on occasion of the Congressional elections. The 1950 elections were unusually bad. After what it called 'a nightmare of immersion in Billingsgate', the *New York Times* declared in an editorial: 'So complete is the character assassination in some cases that those who reach public office will have lost the confidence of the voters who put them there. The most serious of all, perhaps, is that, if this sort of thing continues, it will become increasingly difficult to get decent men and women to stand for public office because of the unjustified abuse suffered en route.'

'When almost everyone is calling everyone else a liar and a thief, the result becomes a standoff. There is, then, no black and white of reputation in the public mind, only a muddy gray.'

In an attempt to bring about some improvement in this disgraceful and self-defeating situation, the Fair Campaign Practices Committee was set up soon after the election of the 81st Congress, by a two-party group. Matters have not been quite as bad since, but how far this is the result of the Committee's work it is difficult to say. Anyone who tries to clean up political campaigns in the United States runs into two very serious difficulties. The first, as a member of the Fair Campaign Practices Committee, Bruce L. Felknor, has pointed out,[3] is that the political party in America has no real control or disciplinary powers over its branches and sub-branches and the second is that the professional campaign managers will stop at nothing to get their men elected. 'He is in the business of *winning* campaigns. He *must* win to stay in business. He comes to politics in the role of a hired killer. What needs to be done, he will do. If the candidate's "image" needs to be changed, he will propose, even fight, to change it. If the opponent's record can be distorted effectively to present him in a false and damaging light, the professional will undertake to do so.'[4]

In 1962 Governor Rockefeller of New York State was a Republican candidate in the Primary elections for the Presidency. The Women's Division of the Democratic Party's State Committee was persuaded to sponsor a large newspaper advertisement, late in the campaign, latched on to the fact that the Governor had been recently divorced and to the rumour that he was about to remarry. The advertisement had a headline declaring: 'Women Don't Want a Part-time Governor Any More than They Want a Part-time Husband'. It then went on to tell readers that the Governor was much too busy doing what it called 'Romancing the White House' to bother his head about problems relating to the State of New York. To drive the lesson home, there was a photograph of Morgenthau, the Democratic candidate, with his family. Against it was the question, 'And where will you find Bob Morgenthau? Why, at home, worrying about the same problems *you* worry about.' The mud had been thrown, and it had stuck.

The American method of arriving at nominations for the Presidency does not strike outside observers as displaying a high degree of seriousness. The televising of party conventions and the repeated appearance of candidates on other kinds of television programmes means that the candidate without popular appeal of the kind that can be communicated on television has practically no chance of success. Such programmes, says a Brookings Institution report, 'have changed the field of combat in ways that probably tend to favour certain personality types as candidates and exclude others. They have paved the way for campaign strategies and tactics that would not otherwise have been possible. They have made any potential candidate occupying the front-runner position with the voters much more conspicuous than he used to be, while also putting the other candidates under strong compulsions to develop counter-strategies emphasising popular appeal. They have opened the national party conventions to popular inspection and in so doing have brought changes in convention behaviour and increased the pressure for other changes.'[5]

There are several important conclusions to be drawn from this. The first is that, as with all television performances, there is a primary and secondary audience. The primary audience consists of the people who actually see the programme; the secondary audience comprises those who read about it afterwards. Viewers will give their main attention to how a person looks; readers will necessarily be chiefly concerned with what he is reported to have said. Since a transcript, which is what a newspaper report is, cannot indicate the light and shade of the original delivery, its tone and texture will be far too even, and to that extent it will be a distortion. A transcript makes everything of equal importance, with no emphases and no throwaways. Yet it may have been precisely these features of a speech which charmed or repelled both the audience on the spot and the much larger audience in front of their television screen.

The wily and experienced practitioner will be aware of this. He will be careful to provide the press with quotable material which will not spoil in the printing and which sub-editors are unlikely to miss. He will preface anything he wants emphasised with such phrases as, 'And let us make no mistake about this', and 'Of one thing we can be absolutely sure', while the approach of a throwaway will be indicated by 'In passing, it's just worth mentioning', or 'Without wanting to make too much of a point of it'. None of this can alter the fact, however, that if he succeeds, if the electors eventually prefer him to his rivals, it will because he is found to be acceptable as a person, not as a producer of noble or brilliant words. He will be the ordinary man writ large, the person who makes the average voter feel good, the Big Leader with whom he can identify himself. In this respect at least the American system of selection, superficially crazy as it may appear to be, usually, but not always, produces very acceptable national leaders. President Carter, in the opinion of one well qualified to judge, is 'a man who has an innate simplicity and dignity, and has a quality that is particularly noticeable in some southerners, even the most humble, which is the gift of knowing who they are from birth, and having absolutely no misgivings about how to act in the presence of tycoons or coalminers, grocers, scholars, paupers, presidents, or kings and queens.'[6] Hubert Humphrey, who had the Democratic nomination for President twice and might well have won the first time, if he had not been up against the formidable power of the Kennedy clan, 'almost exactly resembles one's image of the average American, or perhaps, to locate him more precisely, one's image of the average midwestern senator. His qualities appear to be those which would bring success in American politics. Above all, he really loves the Clambakes, the pressing of the flesh, the labour union dances, the cheery flash of recognition to each of thousands of supporters, that go with a life of politics and campaigning.[7] It is not, perhaps, merely an accident that gave Carter the Presidency while withholding it from Humphrey. The secret may well be that Carter possessed what Humphrey did not, an unmistakable dignity, which allowed him to survive the showbiz vulgarity of American electioneering without despising it. It is impossible to think of any great political leader anywhere whose reputation is likely to survive his death who has not had this essential quality of unshakable inner dignity. It is a rare quality and it marks the truly superior person. President Nixon lacked it, Roosevelt had it, Macmillan had it, Wilson and Callaghan are both without it and, in the Republic of Ireland, Jack Lynch has it.

Once the hustings are over and the President, Prime Minister and their ministerial colleagues are in power, a rather different set of rules applies. Each of the successful figures has the difficult task of seeming a superior animal, worthy of leadership, and yet at the same time honest, simple, approachable, a genuine democrat to his fingertips. Staying in power does not demand the same set of tricks as getting power in the first place. To begin with, the Leader is expected on public occasions to look and sound like the Leader. If he is to reflect his position, he must have a presence; he must look and sound impressive. He must therefore be capable of making speeches which match the occasion. He need not necessarily have written them himself, but he must have the capacity to deliver them convincingly and impressively, bearing in mind that, thanks to television, he may well be seen and heard in fifty countries or more. John Kennedy enjoyed this aspect of his Presidential duties and he was good at it. The born-to-rule manner suited him and he had no objection whatever to the grand style when he felt the occasion demanded it. Such an occasion was his Inaugural Address in 1961, when he declared, in a very fair Churchillian manner – he was a great admirer of Churchill as an orator – that:

> 'We shall pay any price, bear any burden, meet any hardship, now the trumpet summons us again to bear the burden of a long twilight struggle year in and year out, "rejoicing in hope, patient in tribulation", a struggle against the common enemies of man, tyranny, poverty, disease and war itself. Only a few generations have been granted the role of defending freedom in its hour of maximum danger. The energy, the faith and the devotion which we bring to this endeavour will light our country and all who serve it in the glow from the fire that can truly light the world.'

The style suited his particular upbringing and the nation loved it. Like Senator McCarthy, who did not have a patrician background but who had also found a Roman Catholic atmosphere a help in developing his political rhetoric, John Kennedy understood the value of this specially American blend of religious and political language. 'It spoke so clearly to the peculiar American passion for high thinking and low stubbornness, to the national talent for muffling the rattle of cash in a clatter of ideals.'[8] Whether the words owed more to his speechwriters than to himself, Kennedy had the personality and the confidence to carry them off, and he much enjoyed the occasional opportunity to rise above the everyday conversational level. Like Churchill, but very unlike Sir Harold Wilson, he was a born speechmaker. With becoming frankness, Sir Harold admitted that he had to work hard and not particularly willingly at this branch of the master-politician's trade. 'I don't,' he said, 'find political speeches all that easy. I enjoy a speech in the Houses of Parliament. That's the place where I feel it's easiest. I far prefer to answer questions, whether in Parliament, or on radio or television, or in public meetings. I'm not a natural public orator.'[9]

Sir Harold Wilson was only rarely, in fact, an inspirational speaker. He was not made that way. His ability to sway an audience, to touch its emotions, was very limited. But, especially when playing on his home ground in the House of Commons, he could be a gladiator of considerable quality, a skill which has been of great benefit to him during his political career, not least as Prime Minister. He was not a great debater, in the traditional sense, but he had cultivated a ferocious form of repartee which was invaluable to his Party, at a time when the policy of both of the main parties in British politics was remarkably similar. If one could not attack a policy, one could always attack a person, and Wilson had a great talent in this direction. 'When the policies of rival parties are so close as in some cases to be indistinguishable, the capacity to exploit personalities in argument is of supreme value in Parliament, particularly when the morale of one's own side is low. To be able, however falsely, to make an impressive attack on rivals as incompetent, unintelligent and unreliable is to help convince one's own side that it is, whatever the policy failures, more competent than the Opposition. The regularity with which Heath would keep rising to the Prime Minister's bait was a considerable bonus to Wilson.'[10]

If Wilson was not a great orator – the grand tone, the noble theme were not his stock in trade – his speeches could produce quite a powerful effect on the faithful. At his best, he was capable of creating successful mood music, which roused or calmed a Party or Trade Union Conference in the way the occasion demanded. His speeches read badly – there is rarely an intellectual content which is worth serious consideration – but at the time they were delivered they did what was required of them. They sounded, and were, sincere. Sir Harold Wilson was a remarkable optimist and often naive in his beliefs, but he was not the cheat and swindler his opponents made him out to be. He seems to have been that rather uncommon brand of senior politician, the man who really believed his promises. The fact that he so often broke them was usually due to what he would have felt to be an unkind Fate. Promises and forecasts which are improbable and ill-founded at the time they are made are all too likely to prove impossible to keep.

But, over a period of more than fifteen years, his reputation for cleverness undoubtedly helped the Labour Party both to gain and to hold power. To a great extent, it was the cleverness of the sharp, wounding phrase. Wilson had a pronounced streak of maliciousness in his nature. He enjoyed watching the twitches of his victim after an arrow had gone home. His fondness for the surgical and stabbing metaphor is not accidental. There is a long list of such images, covering the whole of his political career.

> 'It was a clean, antiseptic operation, from which Mr. Barber had barely recovered a year later.'
> 'Roy Jenkins tore him apart, calmly and clinically.'
> 'If any sought to plant any knives in my back, I should rapidly find the Left rallying to my support, weapons turned outwards.'
> 'They had first slashed with their razors, and then fainted at the sight of blood.'

As a phrase man, Wilson could be very good: 'I could not understand how any man could have a slipped disc whom Providence had failed to provide with a backbone'; 'The Liberals' proposals would mean a nine-inch tail trying to wag a 300-inch dog'; and he could also be very bad: 'a round robin to all his friends asking them to join the band'; 'Nixon, a man who had been through the political treadmill'; 'He always kept his cards to his chest, pending a high-level confrontation'; and 'To get the mercy corridor working'.

The nearest that Sir Harold ever came to the grand style, a style which the Victorians and Edwardians took for granted that a Prime Minister or anyone aspiring to be a Prime Minister should have at his command was probably his address to the House of Commons at the time of Sir Winston Churchill's death. Here is a fair sample:

> And it is because of this that the words and deeds of Winston Churchill will form part of the rich heritage of our nation and of our time as long as history comes to be written and to be read. Now his pen and his sword are equally at rest. The tempestuous, restless vitality of a man who would have scorned the ease of a peaceful retreat had ended today in quiet, in peace, in stillness. But what every one of us can know is that Winston Churchill's life, his monumental achievements, have enriched forever – not only our nation which he led, not only the world which he bestrode – but the hearts of each of us whose lives he touched with his greatness.[11]

It is, somewhat paradoxically, easier nowadays in America than in Britain to carry off the grand style, or a passable imitation of it. Modern Americans are fonder of long words and complicated expressions than English people are, and it is far from easy to use simple words on a serious occasion of any kind in the United States. The British politician consequently finds himself in a difficult position. He is required to be, at one and the same time, both straightforward, talking the people's language, but also to show himself above the ordinary level of daily affairs, impressive in his power to dominate a situation and to express himself in a way becoming the dignity of his office. Ideally, he should be that impossible person, the superior common man. Since such a creature cannot exist, he has to try to flit from style to style as the situation demands. Like a good bank manager, he has to maintain the correct psychological distance between himself and his customers for every occasion, drawing closer to establish confidence, withdrawing in order to establish discipline. Getting power in the first place, that is, being elected, is a great test of linguistic ability and flexibility. The candidate has to look and sound like all the people he wishes to represent and to be equally acceptable to people of high intelligence and to near-morons, a far from easy task, which demands that rare paragon, the absolutely classless person.

The problem shows itself in many different ways. It is obviously not a matter of words alone. The English have a useful term, Not

Officer Class, often abbreviated to N.O.C. and occasionally extended to Not Officer Class Material. People who are Officer Class are supposed, usually correctly, to possess, as a result of education and family background, a bundle of qualities which makes it easy for them to assume command and to persuade lesser mortals that command has been placed in the right hands. The one-time British Ambassador to Washington, Peter Jay, is Officer Class Material, in a way that his father-in-law, the Labour Prime Minister, is not. The fact that he has been called the cleverest young man in Britain – how does one know or measure such a thing? – is less important in this respect than his manner and accent. He has the appearance of understanding power and taking it as his due. Neither Sir Harold Wilson nor Mr. Callaghan give quite the same impression. Both of them are undoubtedly very fond of power and worked and schemed hard to get it. But, unlike Mr. Jay, they do not sound like officers. Their voices and their subtleties of manner are wrong for the part. English society being what it is – and this is not the place either to attack or defend it – a speech in the grand manner cannot be delivered in a nasal voice with a pronounced Yorkshire accent. One day, perhaps, but not yet.

The political parties in Britain are still divided as much by their voices as by their beliefs and policies. A study of Conservative Members of Parliament and of Conservative candidates soon reveals that a large majority of them have unmistakably Officer Class voices, voices which are by no means uncommon on the Labour benches, too. The ex-Energy Minister, Mr. Wedgwood Benn, for example, has an accent which would, if this were the only quality required, make him a very acceptable member of the Conservative Party. The point is worth making, because, in class-conscious Britain, 'the language of politics' does not mean only what is said; it means also how it is said. People identify with the 'how' quite as much as with the 'what'.

The voices of the present leader of the Conservative Party, Mrs. Margaret Thatcher, and of her two predecessors, Edward Heath and Harold Macmillan, are of great interest in this connection. Mr. Macmillan was, so to speak, born with his accent; it was ringing in his ears, asking to be imitated, from the time he could distinguish words at all. Mr. Macmillan has the genuine English upper-class, officer class voice. Mrs. Thatcher and Mr. Heath, on the other hand, acquired their upper-class accents too late for them to sound genuine. A connoisseur of such matters can spot the difference immediately and so, one suspects, can quite a large proportion of the electorate. The imitation is too perfect, yet the subtleties are missing. How far either of the two politicians concerned are aware of this, it is difficult to say. Mr. Heath, at least, should be, since he has a good musical ear.

The main disadvantage of the accent which is not quite right is that it is liable to give an impression of insincerity, of an actor playing a part. Such a feeling may be entirely unjust and in the two cases instanced it certainly is. There is no reason whatever to think that either Mrs. Thatcher or Mr. Heath have been anything but sincere in their political statements. But, as we have said earlier, the 'how' is as significant as the 'what' in politics. In 1969, Edward Heath was interviewed on television about his own notions of the 'how'. The interviewer was Robin Day and the questions and answers took this form:

Day 'Four years ago this summer I interviewed you the night you were elected Tory leader, and you said on that occasion that you wanted to create a new political language, a language which would strike a chord, strike people's imagination. Do you think, as a leader, you have entirely succeeded in doing that?'
Heath 'Not entirely, no. I've tried very hard and I've tried to put it in terms which would be understood and to show what we were getting at.'
Day 'Would it be fair to say that you personally are much more interested in policy-making and administration than in the gladiatorial, showmanship side of politics?'
Heath 'I think that is probably true. I don't regard the gladiatorial part as having any great value for itself and, again, I think the public thinks it's irrelevant as well.'

Day then turned to a widely heard criticism of Heath, that he was too cold a person to make a satisfactory leader of a modern political party.

Day 'Is the real Ted Heath a man more capable of anger, of passion, of emotion, than might appear from the press or television?'
Heath 'Is it essential to be angry, is it essential to be emotional to be a good leader? I would say no. I would think that those are

things which warp judgement and it is judgement which people want in a leader.'[12]

This may well be true, provided one inserts the word 'most' between 'people' and 'want'. The electorate does expect its leaders to possess common sense and to show good judgement. But people in a position of power are also required to pay at least a good deal of attention to the morale of their fellow-citizens. Leaders are rightly expected to care as well as explain and justify, to possess a heart as well as a head, which is not at all the same thing as wearing one's heart on one's sleeve. In any case, it is more essential, in life as well as politics, to be sensitive to other people's feelings, opinions and prejudices than to express one's own. The insensitive politician will inevitably commit errors of judgement. One cannot be sensitive by proxy, except in the most crude and unsatisfactory way. Opinion surveys and research assistants who summarise and analyse letters from constitutents are not the same thing as meeting real people, talking to them oneself and trying to understand their problems by listening to them, seeing how they are dressed, and watching the expression on their faces. Any politician who believes that all the important things about people can be stored in a computer will find himself faced with an unpleasant surprise sooner or later.

The higher a politician rises, the more likely it is that he will have little direct contact with the people whom he is supposed to represent and whose lives he in some degree controls. This tendency is just as strongly marked on the Left as on the Right. During the General Election campaign of 1974, a member of Harold Wilson's staff who toured the country with him told a BBC reporter, 'He just seems incapable of communicating'. The reporter added, 'He is so cocooned from actual contact with the people. He relies entirely on advice from a very small ring of confidants. The problem is that, so close are they to Mr. Wilson, so worshipping are they of his every glance in their direction, they tell him only what he wants to know. This gives him a totally false idea of reality.'[13]

Edward Heath – and he is certainly not unique among contemporary politicians – appears to have believed that a Prime Minister, like any other minister or head of department, is essentially a manager. If he has all the available facts, he should be able to make the correct decision. If he makes a wrong decision, he must have been supplied with insufficient or misleading information. Perhaps it all depends on how one defines information.[14]

Holding the view he did, that a person speaks or writes in order to communicate facts, he was bound to produce a certain kind of speech, a statement, and to be very vulnerable to goading opponents, such as Harold Wilson, whose prime aim in putting a question or making an intervention was to make him look ridiculous, not to elucidate further information from him. And the leader who looks ridiculous is soon lost.

Mr. Heath is a serious-minded man who believes that politics is, or should be, a serious matter. Being Prime Minister is strictly comparable with running a large business, and a Prime Minister's utterances should be those which would become a managing director, sober, factual, honest, intelligible and reliable. Humour, ridicule and gladiatorial behaviour of any kind are unseemly and out of place. The quiet manner and firm tone are what is required, and this, from Edward Heath, is what the public has always had. His sense of duty and his belief in following the facts wherever they might happen to lead him ended his career as Prime Minister. The following passage illustrates both his strength and his weakness. It comes from a television interview which took place shortly before Mr. Heath decided to fight a General Election as a result of his unsuccessful battle with the miners. He had been discussing the part played in this struggle by Mr. McGahey, the Communist Vice-President of the National Union of Miners, and went on:

> I think what Mr. McGahey made absolutely plain is that he is regarding this as a political matter. And those of us who have taken part in these negotiations, or in talks with the National Union of Mineworkers, have known this from the beginning. He has made it quite plain over the weekend, as has another miners' leader, that the object of what they are doing is not a wage negotiation. It is not to get a settlement of a claim in accordance with Stage Three – and by that, I mean smashing what is accepted as fair now by five million people, and approved by Parliament, to get rid of the elected Government of the day. Now that is entirely a political approach and he has said quite openly that he wishes to do it in order to get a left-wing Government. Obviously he then expects a left-wing Government to toe the line so far as he is concerned. It is very good that that has been made quite plain.'[15]

The analysis is clear, the facts correct, the presentation straightforward. Yet Mr. Heath lost the battle, because he underestimated the strength of the organised working-class opposition to the Conservatives, and in particular to any statutory control of wages or curbing of trade union power. His computer had failed him.

Heath has a good mind, of a special type, a managing director's mind. The present Prime Minister, Mr. James Callaghan, is cast in an entirely different mould.

> His is a crude and limited, and rather pedestrian and unprincipled mind, and his utterances and actions reflect that fact.... He has no difficulty in handling subordinates; rather the crude confidence of a man habitually rude to waiters. With those he knows to be his equals or suspects of possessing greater intellectual attainments, he is curiously gauche. Television news film alone demonstrates how he deals with foreign statesmen: he bows and grins frequently and is constantly touching his guests, rather like an over-solicitous butler guiding them on their way.[16]

Despite these limitations – they are those of the senior non-commissioned officer, which Mr. Callaghan was – the Prime Minister has a quality which is invaluable, if not indispensable, in modern politics, a sure sense of what his rank and file supporters are feeling and the ability to translate that into words of the right flavour. 'Throughout his public life,' Patrick Cosgrave wrote when the new Prime Minister took up office, 'Mr. Callaghan has been expert at giving banal utterance to Labour's gut feelings'.[17]

One would be hard put to discover passages or even phrases of any distinction in the Prime Minister's speeches. His speciality has always been what one analyst, Michael Wood, has excellently described as 'a very flexible form of straight talk', adding that such language is 'a very valuable gift for a politician'.[18] It can be easily illustrated by a reply given by Mr. Callaghan in the House of Commons to one of his own colleagues, the much more radically inclined Mrs. Judith Hart. The subject was Rhodesia and Mr. Callaghan gave this assurance:

> We have no intention of going into Rhodesia to try to pull somebody's chestnuts from the fire, or to monitor the proposals. What we must be ready to do if there is an agreement which is acceptable to all those shades of opinion in Rhodesia I have outlined – if necessary at some sacrifice to ourselves – is to assist in

ensuring that that settlement is translated into reality for all the people of that country.[19]

At a first glance, and even more probably at a first hearing, this seems plain and straightforward enough. It has the flavour of 'straight talk', but, as Mr. Wood pointed out, careful examination reveals that it is really far from straight. 'Flexibility', that is, vagueness, abounds. Does 'we have no intention of going into Rhodesia' mean 'we shall not send troops into Rhodesia'? Does 'ready to do' mean 'shall do'? What is the significance of 'at some sacrifice to ourselves'? Would the sacrifice be of money, human lives, reputation, or what? Does 'translated into reality' mean 'enforced'? It is small wonder that Mrs. Hart was not fully satisfied.

Evasiveness is a normal part of politics and it may take one of many forms, along a spectrum which ranges from the downright lie at one end to a polite no at the other. Nothing could be briefer, more pointed and yet at the same time more polite than some of the Oral Answers in the House of Commons. The Minister will not be drawn, and he says so very plainly.

Mr. Raymond Fletcher, for example, asked the Secretary of State for Foreign Affairs 'if he will consider the progressive abolition of the Diplomatic Service and its replacement by a purely Consular Service, in view of the declining importance of ambassadorial functions and duties'.

Mr. Mulley   No, sir.
Mr. Fletcher   I thank my Right Honourable Friend for that slap in the face.[20]

During the Cuban missile crisis the American press became increasingly angry about what was politely called 'managed news' from the White House. This was a euphemism for 'bare-faced lies', and Arthur Sylvester, Assistant Secretary of Defense for Public Affairs made matters worse by explaining that Government officials had a right and indeed a duty to lie if the nation were threatened with nuclear destruction. The point has not often been made quite so plainly, but the matter did the reputation of the Kennedy administration no good at all.

President Johnson wisely preferred the vague statement to the plain lie, but even this got him into trouble more than once. In a speech made on 21st February 1964, in California, the President said that the countries – China and North Vietnam – which were supporting the Communist guerillas in South Vietnam were playing what he described as a 'deeply dangerous game'. Reporters were told by Pierre Salinger, on behalf of the White House, that they could assume this meant that the United States would, if they deemed it necessary, carry the war into the North and perhaps to China itself. This produced such a hostile public reaction – another Korean situation appeared to be in the making – that the Secretary of State was obliged to call a news conference in order to deny that the war would be pushed into North Vietnam. President Johnson made a pained statement to the effect that he was mystified to know how the newsmen could possibly have interpreted his words in the way they had.

News conferences, an American invention, are rarely, from the point of view of the public and the media, very satisfactory affairs, although with a good performer there can be a certain sporting interest in watching the central figure fending off his questioners and keeping the proceedings under his control. These conferences nearly always begin with a carefully prepared statement, which may or may not embody the personal feelings of the person who reads it. The skill then consists of providing the newsmen with no more information than is contained in the statement and in using the questions as a form of market research. The new conference gives a splendid opportunity for cultivating the art of saying nothing in an agreeable and interesting way.

An American President is expected to show competence in his handling of these conferences. Other heads of state are not required to possess quite the same talent, except occasionally on television, when the number of people involved is likely to be much smaller. Any kind of press conference is essentially a set piece, with a great deal of ritual about it, but it can, even so, be important in giving a first airing to a newsworthy policy statement. John Kennedy, for instance, chose this way of making known his Government's view on Laos and on the action of the American steel companies in raising prices by $6 a ton at a time when the United States was experiencing economic difficulties at home and political crises abroad. In the first instance the statement[21] began with a quiet explanation: 'Laos was one of the new states which had recently emerged from the French union and it was the clear premise of the 1954 settlement that this new country would be neutral, free of external domination by anyone.'

Then there came a declaration of policy: 'First, we strongly and unreservedly support the goal of a neutral and independent Laos. Secondly, if there is to be a peaceful situation, there must be a cessation of the present armed attacks by externally supported Communists.'

The Secretary of State might have expressed himself in exactly similar terms. The President's statement at the second conference,[22] however, contained a much more personal element. The President was angry and intended to show it: 'The American people will find it hard, as I do, to accept a situation in which a tiny handful of steel executives, whose pursuit of power and profit exceed their sense of public responsibility, can show such utter contempt for the interests of 185 million Americans.'

It was occasions such as this, thoroughly publicised, which allowed Americans of both parties to identify themselves with the Presidency to an extent which had never happened before. The President had come to personify political issues. With skilful public relations help, he was able to build himself up into a Galahad-like figure, a role which he did not entirely deserve. Miracles were performed in keeping his public and private life strictly apart and his image as a superhumanly active, wise, far-seeing leader of his people was at its brightest by the time he was assassinated. The man had style and a nation will still, fortunately, respond to style. President Nixon had power but no style and his speechwriters, ever obliging and understanding of his limitations, produced words to match, a tinny echo of the grand style for a tinny President:

> Let us accept that high responsibility to build a structure of peace not as a burden but gladly, gladly because the chance to build such a peace is the noblest endeavour a people can engage in, gladly also because only if we act greatly, meeting our responsibilities abroad, will we remain a great nation and only if we remain a great nation will we act greatly in meeting our challenges at home.[23]

For a national leader to get himself associated with a successful slogan can be advantageous, unless and until the slogan, like the Conservative 'You've Never Had It So Good', goes sour. American Presidents like to have a slogan with which to label their administration. Franklin D. Roosevelt had his New Deal, Harry Truman his Fair Deal, John Kennedy his New Frontier and

Lyndon Johnson his Great Society, 'a place where every child can find knowledge to enrich his mind and to enlarge his talents. It is a place where leisure is a welcome chance to build and to reflect, not a feared cause of boredom and restlessness. It is place where the city of man serves not only the needs of the body and the demands of commerce, but the desire for beauty and the hunger for community. It is a place where man can renew contact with nature.'[24]

To some observers, this did not seem to relate very closely to the America they knew, but it was a nice idea and did nobody any harm. It was a kind of senior statesman's poetry. To those – a very small minority on either side of the Atlantic – who are familiar with real poetry, the Lyndon B. Johnson variety may seem a trifle sentimental and lacking in originality. Millions, however, would not see it that way. It brings a shaft of sunlight and hope into their lives and that, after all, is one way for a national leader to succeed. Both politicians and advertising agencies are in the poetry business for a good deal of the time, and both knock the life out of the poetic vocabulary pretty fast. Many good words, as David Watt has shrewdly and tolerantly pointed out, 'have died in a cause which has to be our cause whether we like it or not, namely popular democracy. You cannot conduct a popular democracy without wearing out words.'[25]

4 Language as Group-cement

Politicians are all the time looking both outwards and inwards, outwards to the general public whose support is ultimately essential and inwards towards their own colleagues. Any analysis of political language which is limited to a consideration of bridges between, say, the Member of Parliament and his constituents is dealing with only half the story. The jargon, the tricks of style, the in-references, the conventions which bind fellow Parliamentarians and fellow-Party members together are equally important, both as a feature of the national life and as a field of academic study. When Neil Postman says that 'in a democratic society, the language of politics has as one of its main purposes the clear statement of practical, alternative ways of living',[1] he is describing an ideal situation which is sadly unlike any with which we are so far familiar. A 'statement' implies that information is set out in a cool, objective, comprehensible fashion, for people to ponder over seriously, slowly and quietly. There is remarkably little political language of this kind about. Would that there were. To discover examples of contemporary political 'statement' which are not to some degree emotionally or strategically loaded is a difficult task. Politicians themselves do not usually behave in this way, although outside observers of the political scene may do so from time to time.

What, in any case, does 'practical, alternative ways of living' mean? In the United States, do the Republicans and Democrats seriously offer 'practical, alternatives ways of living'? To gain power, they may well suggest this is the case – the matter of product differentiation has already been discussed in Chapter Two – but how far does reality eventually bear out the promise? What is the 'practical, alternative way of living' which the Labour Party is likely to inaugurate which will be distinct from anything the Conservatives can offer or provide? Whichever party is in power, houses will have to be built, bought, heated and lit; people will have to be clothed, fed, doctored and buried; children will have to be reared and educated; taxes will have to be paid; food will have to be grown and processed. The party approaches to these basic aspects of being alive can only be minimally different. Funerals may be dealt with by the municipality or by private firms; taxation may be direct or indirect; television sets may be bought or rented; motorcars may be easy or difficult to get; government departments and public services may be efficient or inefficient.

In today's circumstances, when the atmosphere is conditioned, and, as some might say, poisoned by ideologies and counter-ideologies, man is not supposed to live by reality alone. The theory, the ideology, is supposed in some mysterious way to transform the reality, so that if the London Underground system provides an equally bad public service under a Labour Government as under a Conservative Government, or vice versa, the badness is in some way less bad, more excusable, more tolerable because it is taking place along the road to socialism or in pursuit of Conservative principles. What actually happens day by day looks different, sometimes very different, according to whether one is wearing spectacles manufactured by the Left or the Right. The parties are, in fact, primarily in business to make and sell pairs of spectacles, not to provide 'clear statements of practical, alternative ways of living'. And they are concerned quite as much with running a closely-knit company, with a 100 per cent loyal, fully indoctrinated staff and no industrial disputes, as with selling the goods they produce. One of the principal tools for ensuring this is the Party language, which binds member to member and helps to create and maintain the necessary Cowboys and Indians, Cops and Robbers, line-up. Political bodies, like doctors, lawyers, journalists and professional sportsmen, use special forms of language to create a group solidarity and to present a unified front to the outside world.

Let us consider in this connection a series of examples taken from the world of Trade Unionism, from speeches made at the annual Trades Union Congress, when most delegates ooze orthodoxy at every pore. Here, to begin with, is the Engineers leader, Hugh Scanlon, during a debate on the Industrial Relations Act.

> *Quotation 1*   'Even after that week in July of this year when the five dockers were released because of the mighty upsurge of industrial solidarity'[2]
>
> *Quotation 2*   'Enough, and more than enough, has been said and written about the intervention of law into industrial relations, but if workers always obeyed class legislation we would not be in this

hall today, because there would be no trade union movement.'[3]

Quotation 3 'The Act has given carte blanche to small employers to use the law as a battleground against the Labour Movement. These small fry on the fringes of industrial life take up legal bludgeons against organised Labour'.[4]

Mr. Scanlon is a practised operator, with a lifetime's experience of bringing fellow Trade Unionists over to his way of thinking. He knows the phrases to make the heart beat faster, to persuade an audience that brother is speaking to brother, that the enemies are all around and that the sword must never sleep in its scabbard. So, in the passages given above, we have 'the mighty upsurge of industrial solidarity' (organised trade unions created disturbances and threatened to go on strike); 'the intervention of law into industrial relations' (the attempt by the Government to prevent the Trade Unions from being a law unto themselves); 'class legislation' (laws passed by Parliament which restrict the powers of Trade Unions. Penal death duties, a wealth tax or discrimination against self-employed people are not, of course, examples of class legislation, because they are aimed from below upwards); 'these small fry on the fringes of industrial life' (independent firms with fewer than a thousand people, the firms which still employ most of the nation's work-force); 'take up legal bludgeons against organised Labour' (refuse to be dictated to by the Trade Unions).

This, by any definition, is political language. It is not, one hopes, the language which Mr. Scanlon employs when conversing with his wife and friends, although one can never be sure of this. It is extremely unlikely to make converts and it is not in fact intended to do so. Its aim is to put heart into workers wearing their Trade Union hats – 'the lads' – and to cause the other side – 'the bosses' – to shudder, tremble and, with reasonable luck, capitulate.

Mr. Briginshaw, of the National Society of Operative Printers, Graphical and Media Personnel (surely one of the most oddly named trade unions in Britain) is an equal master of this kind of we're-all-in-the-fight-together language. At the same meeting of the TUC he laid these offerings on the altar.

Quotation 1 'When the Tories are in Government, they provide an impossible context for the trade unions in this country, shackled by repressive legislation, to meet their great historic tasks.'[5]

Quotation 2 'We listened to Wedgwood Benn yesterday. It was a good speech, but I think, for the record, we ought to say to Wedgy that neither the problems of this country nor the problems of the working people can wait for general elections.'[6]

Mr. Briginshaw speaks the Trade Union language as well as Mr. Scanlon does. They are both admirably fluent in it. So we have 'the Tories' (abusive word for the Conservatives); 'shackled by repressive legislation' (required to observe the ordinary law of the land); 'great historical tasks' (becoming the controlling force in British politics); 'Wedgy' (Mr. Wedgwood Benn); 'problems of the working people' (wage demands).

Delegates to the TUC and the Labour Party Conference expect to hear this language. They cheer it and they are cheered by it. It is their common tongue, their rallying call. The generous use of Christian names and even of shortened and familiar forms of Christian names contributes to the effect.

Chairman I will now have to call on Barbara to reply.
Barbara Castle One paper this morning carried the headline, 'Jennie saves Barbara'. You know, this is not a question of saving Barbara, or any other members of the Executive, or any member of the Government. What we are debating today is how to save our Movement from tearing itself apart. And so I hope you will be patient with me if I try to do justice to the innumerable points that have been raised in the debate.

Now listening to the debate and to all the speeches, I have been trying to disentangle the threads of the argument. Take the support for Composite 22; we had Frank first of all explaining that his composite had only to do with legislation, and he said, nothing to do with the argument as to whether we need a prices and incomes policy. Jack Cooper came along and said his union would support it, yet believed that we must have a prices and incomes policy. But finally we had Hughie Scanlon coming along, rejecting the whole philosophy of what the Government was trying to do. Now Danny McGarvey said he hoped he would not have any double talk from Barbara.[7]

Jennie and Barbara and Frank and Jack and Hughie and Danny. It is all very cosy and friendly, with the linked-arms singing of the Internationale at the conclusion of it all. Occasionally – very occasionally nowadays – someone, usually a woman, rises in her seat to blow away the jargon and the empty rhetoric for a few golden minutes with a little plain speaking. Here, for instance, is Miss Veitch, of the National Union of General and Municipal Workers telling the assembled delegates at the TUC that it is high time they put some muscle behind the pious resolutions on equal pay for women which they pass year after year, as part of the Congress ritual.

> I have seen women in photographic plants working on components which have made the head of a pin look clumsy. I have seen them winding wire which is half the thickness of a hair. They were young women. They needed to be, for they had to have a high level of visual acuity, and they needed aptitude and dexterity in manual skills, observation and concentration. You know, some people talk about cruelty to battery hens. Much more should they be concerned for women and girls in factories, who suffer from the pressure of speed and the discipline of exacting and monotonous work. We want these things taken into account. Let me say that women are not fools; they do not expect equal pay to be realised overnight. But neither are they stooges; you cannot kid them for ever. They want the beginning of the implementation of equal pay, and they want it now.[8]

This is miles away from 'the mighty upsurge of industrial solidarity', 'repressive class legislation' and the rest of the froth and pomposity which befouls and corrupts Labour politics today. Fifty years ago there was none of it and very little twenty-five years ago. It has spread in from Communist ideology, journalism and speech-making since the end of the Second World War and a number of the old-timers in both the Labour Party and the unions learnt and absorbed it during their Communist and near-Communist days. It is curious that, although there has been a great deal of talk about the infiltration of Communists and Communist ideas into the trade unions and the Labour Party, practically no comment has been made about the infiltration of Communist language, which is just as insidious and in some ways more so. To use another man's jargon, unless one does so in inverted commas, is to have sat at the table with him, eaten his food and found it to one's taste.

If one is accustomed to read Communist books, pamphlets and newspapers, it is easy to spot the key words and the flavour in a second when these characteristics appear in a completely different context, when one could easily be off one's guard. There is, for instance, no reason to suppose that W. Page, of the National Union of Agricultural and Allied Workers, is or ever has been a member of the Communist Party, but during a debate at the TUC he asked this question: 'How long would a building worker, working in difficult conditions, have to work to pick up the money that is picked up in a few minutes in some plush office by the slick operators of land speculation?'

This is the Communist way of saying, 'picked up in a few minutes by a land speculator'. One may compare the use of 'plush lounges' in the following Left-wing note on sinister enemy tactics: 'In July executives from 36 multinational companies met in the plush lounges of Geneva's Hotel Intercontinental to plan an investment strategy for Black Africa.'[9]

'Met at the Intercontinental Hotel, Geneva' would not be the same at all. The multinationals have to be castigated for sitting on thicker, softer cushions than other people, with their feet on more silent, more expensive carpets, and with plenty of big mirrors around to watch for the approach of enemies and eavesdroppers. The delegates almost certainly met in no such room, but 'plush lounges' gives the right impression of the decadent, spendthrift habits which Left-wing folklore associates with large companies and the expression is instinctively and automatically used on such an occasion as this. Communist propagandist are much given to this kind of compound noun. The office of any capitalist concern is not just an office; it is a plush-office. One can feel the invisible, essential hyphen between the two words. Similarly, a financier or developer cannot be merely an operator; he has to be a slick-operator. One is reminded of the estate agents' luxury flats and the travel agents' luxury cruises.

An examination of two avowedly Communist newspaper articles will help to make the point clearer. The first concerns a strike at Leyland Motors, where workers were told that, despite a much larger claim, they were going to get no more than the 10 per cent permitted by the Government. They were further informed that, unless industrial relations and productivity greatly improved at Leyland, the National Enterprise Board would put no more money into the company. At that point the strikers decided to go back, a step which an outside observer might consider very sensible. The Communist press, however, spoke of 'blackmail', the official Communist word for causing a group of workers to do what the Communist Party does not want them to do, for being reasonable and co-operative, in fact.

So, in this case, 'British Leyland's truck and bus workers at Leyland were blackmailed into going back to work and accepting the 10 per cent limit and management's productivity deal'.[10] This, inevitably, was after 'angry scenes at the mass meeting', when there was a two to one vote for a return to work. 'The National Enterprise Board,' declared the paper, 'and behind them the Labour Government, tried to blackmail us into going back to work. Our full-time officials accepted being blackmailed and forced our shop stewards to accept it.' And, to prove that the money to pay a 30 per cent increase was really there all the time, 'the Bus and Truck Division of British Leyland made £21 million profit last year'.

'Blackmail' in this context means two things, that the men were told firmly that at 10 per cent was the maximum permitted by the Government and that it was impressed on them that, if the situation at Leyland failed to show a substantial and rapid change for the better, money would run out, the company would have to close down and there would be no jobs for anyone. To point this out is, in Communist language, 'blackmail'. Any thought that an industrial concern has to have a surplus of income over expenditure in order to have funds to invest in development is brushed aside as capitalist nonsense. Any surplus is automatically labelled 'profit' and should be returned to the workers straight away.

These two words, 'blackmail' and 'profit' are highly important weapons in the Left's political armoury. Anyone who uses them in the right way is immediately identifiable as a friend and a brother. They are passwords to comradeship and trust. To threaten to cut off the nation's supplies of petrol and electricity in support of an outrageous pay-claim is not, of course, blackmail. Another keyword is 'mob'. The Conservative Party does not exist; there is only 'Thatcher's mob'. Non-Communists do not eat; they 'gorge themselves on their four-course lunch'. And, even worse than the capitalists, bosses and luxury-livers, are the racists, a word for which no adequate definition has yet been found. Any attempt to discover an agreed meaning for it is likely to land one in considerable trouble, the argument being that, since all decent and right-thinking people know instinctively what a racist is, anyone who starts asking questions is a saboteur and clearly on the side of the racists. The Nazis used the word 'Jew' in a very similar way and the Victorians sorted their fellow-citizens out with 'atheist' and 'agnostic'. To the Communists, 'racist' came as a most valuable addition to the emergency verbal rations which every loyal and prudent member of the Party should carry in his knapsack. Here is a very choice example of the term in use: 'It is now vital that all democratic and progressive forces turn their attention to the activities of the racists among the youth and, as Tom Bell, YCL General Secretary, put it at the Red Festival, "we shall not rest until this infant Frankenstein offspring of fascism is politically smothered in its cradle and sent to an early grave"'.[11]

One has to be very well schooled in Communist theology and liturgy to be able to write like that. But it is an essentially religious language, meaningful only to the faithful, and irritating and puzzling to anyone else.

Is there any corresponding jargon on the political Right, words and phrases which make for group solidarity and which have no place or use on the Left? The short answer is no, but this needs a good deal of qualification. As we have said earlier, Right tends to be distinguished from Left more by accent than by words, although this test is far from infallible. Political jargon is to a great extent the product of an ideology and, although there may be a Conservative philosophy, there is no Conservative ideology. The bond between members of the parties of the Centre and the Right, the Liberals and Conservatives in Britain, is a common suspicion and rejection of the policies and actions of the Left. It has no considerable body of jargon of its own to set against the neo-Marxist and crypto-Communist vocabulary of the Left.

This does not mean that there is nothing about a Conservative speech which tells us, from its style and from the speaker's choice of this word or phrase rather than another, that it is a Conservative talking. Here is a small anthology of Conservative thumbprints, all taken from the Report of the 1976 Party Conference. The names of the speakers are deliberately withheld here, to encourage concentration on the words themselves, but the page reference is given, so that anyone who longs to break through the anonymity may look up the missing details for himself.

First thumbprint 'There will still be need for supplementary benefits and there will still be people who will continue to try to live as parasites. But the opportunities will not be there for the fiddling to take place on anything like the present scale, and much of the money saved – some £200 million a year is mentioned as the present level – will be used as direct aid to the genuinely needy. For those who continue to scrounge I would hope that provision can be made for payment of rent and rates to the local authority and for swindlers to have their cash handouts replaced by vouchers for food and clothing for a period of time relative to their fraud.'[12]

Second thumbprint 'We have become a soft, woolly society. Too many pathetic excuses are afforded to criminals and too little to the unfortunate victims. People are frustrated by the laxness shown towards crime in general and its undermining of the whole moral fabric of our society. Penal measures are failing to reflect the type of punishments which the majority consider necessary to protect society and many blame the police for their non-enforcement of the law.

'But it is not the fault of the police now. We have too many self-righteous, self-appointed, self-styled do-gooders trying to undermine the system. It is up to us to give the police our support and defend them against these crafty, conniving menaces who are relentlessly striving to destroy our society by focusing attention upon petty police abuses. We have a marvellous police force and their physical courage is unequalled.

'Attached to this there is another way in which the demand for discipline is appearing. It is in the widening belief that there is inadequate discipline through the whole of our educational system. Hooliganism, theft, violence to other pupils, violence to teachers, as well as illiteracy and academic failures are associated particularly with the large inner-city comprehensive schools. People are now coming to realise that the permissive society depends for its fragile stability on spending the capital of the discipline of the past.'[13]

Third thumbprint 'Fundamentally we must abolish the domestic rate, reduce the commercial and empty property rates and replace them not with a tax on property, which has proved to be a broken reed, but with a tax payable by all who are able to use the services provided, that is to say, all voters in the area of a local authority. Such a tax would be cheap, fair and certain. It would undoubtedly be accompanied by a generous rebate scheme to exempt those on lower incomes. My estimate of the level of such a tax would be not more than £50 per person per year – in other words, every voter would pay £1 per week for all local services.'[14]

Fourth thumbprint 'I will tell you what we cannot afford. We cannot afford more pay for less work. We cannot afford a combination of high tax rates and loose social security regulations that make it more profitable to stay at home than go to work. We cannot afford subsidies that go to rich as well as poor, to those families that can well afford to pay for their own food and their own housing. We cannot afford not to sell council houses. We cannot afford to go on building endless subsidised council houses when more people would much prefer to buy their own homes.'[15]

If these four passages were mixed up with four equally typical extracts of about the same length from the proceedings of the TUC or the Labour Party Conference, there would be very little difficulty in deciding which came from the Left and which from the Right. But what clues should we be following? What gives the four pieces quoted above their specifically Conservative flavour? It is not the use of an ideological vocabulary, comparable with that of the Marxists. What characterises much of Conservative speaking and writing is plain statement on topics where straightforward, direct language is out of fashion. Left-wing politicians would never say the following things in public, although they might well think them:

'We cannot afford more pay for less work'
'We cannot afford subsidies that go to rich as well as poor, to those families which can well afford to pay for their own food and their own housing'
'. . . a tax on property, which has proved to be a broken reed'
'a tax payable by all who are able to use the services provided'
'There is inadequate discipline through the whole of our educational system'
'We have a marvellous police force'

It is not that such statements are foolish or untrue. On the contrary, they are the conclusions to which any unprejudiced observer might well be likely to come. But they reflect thoughts which are anathema to members of the Left and to those who consider it important not to antagonise them. The Left, for reasons which are not always entirely clear, does believe, or pretends to believe, that we can, as a nation, afford more pay for less work; does not agree that those who can afford to meet the full cost of their food and housing should do so; will not go along with the idea that rates, i.e. a tax on property, should be replaced by a residential tax; disapproves of the notion of discipline in schools; and hates and despises the police as a matter of course.

Consequently, in today's political climate, anyone who makes the kind of remarks that have just been quoted is immediately identified as a Tory, a reactionary and an enemy of the working-class, if not of the human race as a whole. Equally, any two people who are prepared to give public utterance to such appalling heresies as 'we cannot afford more pay for less work' have automatically forged a bond of friendship and brotherhood with one another. They have thought the unthinkable and uttered the unspeakable and, worse still, they have uttered it plainly and without shame.

There are, however, different brands of Conservative language, all making for group solidarity and mutual trust and affection. Rhetoric and jargon are not the prerogative of the Left, as one can see from one of the speeches at the 1977 Conservative Conference, made by Mrs. Rosemary Brown. Mrs. Brown was moving a resolution calling for changes in the law concerning the closed shop. In the course of this address she said:

'The British rail workers aren't isolated victims. Almost every week someone somewhere is being sacrificed to union tyranny. Is it right that a man whose contract never stipulated union membership should be conscripted into joining or sacked without compensation, without right of appeal, without any redress against unfair dismissal? The price of nonconformity can be a life sentence in the Siberia of unemployment.

'We aren't just talking about non-joiners. Equally chilling, what of those who are expelled or refused entry? In Clive Jenkins' vernacular, if the union does not like the colour of your eyes, then you enter the wonderland world of big brother knows best. An appeal set up by the unions with no legal standing, no teeth to impose justice, a hanging jury.

'The tentacles of union power are clawing into even the smallest firms, blackmailing them into submission as a sheer condition of survival. Was this the aim of the millions of working people who signed up, as I did, believing they were joining a voluntary movement? Is this what we want – closed-shop Britain?'[16]

This is the Conservative shouting style, the voice of the platform orator anywhere, not the quiet voice of reason. Its jargon and slogans are little different in character and quality from those which the Left uses with enthusiasm on similar occasions – 'sacrificed to union tyranny'; 'a life sentence in the Siberia of unemployment'; 'the wonderland world of big brother knows best'; 'a hanging jury'; 'the tentacles of union power'; 'blackmailing them into submission'; 'closed-shop Britain'. It is interesting to observe that 'blackmailing' belongs to the vocabulary of both Left and Right and it would need only a slight twist and easy translation to make this particular Conservative speech perfectly acceptable at the TUC. The fact that Mrs. Brown does not like the unions is clear and no doubt she found much sympathy for her views at the Conservative Conference. But there is nothing specifically Conservative about her style. If the speech was loudly applauded, as indeed it was, this was because of its sentiments, not for any masonic, tribal features in its language. Mrs. Brown is the kind of person who is useful to any political party. She is a good mob-orator, and that is certainly not a talent to be despised. It is saleable on both sides of the political fence.

The social peculiarities of Conservatism are quite another matter. The conversations which take place at Conservative fêtes, garden parties and wine and cheese parties have been caricatured enough for most people to be aware of their general tone and of the comic possibilities in certain key phrases, and habits of intonation, pronounciation and stressing. The fact that one breed of Conservative converses in exceptionally loud voices is also easily observable and familiar. The hunting, point-to-pointing Conservative, too, has come in for his and her fair share of attention, from satirists and hostile critics. The closed world, the sub-culture of well-to-do, well-connected Conservatives, of both the urban and rural varieties, is, at the same time, a comfort and a misfortune to those who manage the Party's affairs, a comfort because it is always encouraging to know that one has a solid core of supporters who can be guaranteed to vote the right way, no matter what the circumstances, and a misfortune because it does a modern political party no good to have too many friends who look and sound like yesterday that is almost too good to be true.

The more influential and successful Conservatives, like their equivalents on the Labour side, are much given to writing their memoirs, and in these volumes it is possible for the uninitiated to obtain a fair impression of the strange private language which is exchanged between one notable and another. A good example of best-people communication is the following letter written by Lord Salisbury to the Earl of Kilmuir:

'My dear David,
   May I most respectfully congratulate you? By Jove, that *was* a good speech, closely reasoned, powerful, and, especially in the closing passages, extremely moving. The best I ever heard you make.
                                                        Yours ever,
                                                        Bobbety'[17]

This letter, somewhat unbelievably, was written only twenty years ago. Faced with the problem of guessing the date, anyone could be excused for saying 1880 or 1910. The fact that the two men were on David and Bobbety terms is a matter of no particular importance. Members of the Labour political élite write to one another in not dissimilar terms, although 'Bobbety' has, it is true, a fairly distinctive Conservative flavour about it. A Left-wing Bobbety is not easy to imagine. But the whole tone of the letter, which has the period-piece 'By Jove' to add the final touch of perfection, is True Blue. It could belong nowhere else. The fact that Lord Kilmuir chooses to publish it is also revealing. His *Memoirs* provide fresh evidence of what one already had good grounds to suspect, that a well-developed sense of humour is not often found among successful politicians. Wit and occasionally buffoonery, yes, but not humour. A person endowed with a keen awareness of the human comedy and of the absurdity of taking oneself too seriously, is unlikely to go into politics in the first place. If he does, he will not survive very long. A common quality of politicians, no matter what their creed, is an exceptional ability to take themselves and their calling very seriously indeed. Lord Kilmur ('the world of politics entranced me') assuredly had this quality and as a result he had no difficulty in writing and speaking in a way which must cause most non-political animals to marvel.

'The politician must live always at the top of his form. He must study his profession with care, and be prepared for disasters. He must practise the art of speaking, whether on a lorry in the pouring rain to a dozen surly and unimpressed electors; in a bored or angry House of Commons; at an infinite number and variety of public dinners; or in the Cabinet or committees, where claptrap in any form is fatal. One vital test of the successful politician is that you can put him in any place and tell him to make a speech and it would be perfectly attuned to the mood or circumstance of the audience – without losing its own purpose. This is partly intuitive, but principally the result of assiduous attention to the politician's trade. Words, whether spoken or written, are his only weapons; he must learn to master them, to deploy them dexterously; they must enrage, placate, amuse, or sober as circumstances demand.[18]

This is surely just a little too good to be true, yet there is no reason to suppose that the author was writing it with his tongue in his check. Who, one may ask is the extraordinary, superhuman creature whom Lord Kilmuir describes, trained to the minute and always at the top of his form, perfectly attuned to every mood of every audience, never deviating an inch from his purpose, no matter how great the aggravation or the temptation? How could one ever believe in his existence or even think of him without a smile? Gradually the suspicion grows that politics may be some odd kind of freemasonry of the humourless, that politicians lack some essential human quality. If this were true, then the fundamental resemblances between them would be more important than the differences cutting across party divisions and making even the most ferocious of verbal battles little more than the playful antics of tiger cubs.

There may be something in this argument. It amounts to saying that all footballers or soldiers or jockeys or actors understand one another, even though their livelihood may depend on constant rivalry in public and on a need to do everything possible to beat one's opponent. They are held together by a common language and a common set of rules, and very often by a considerable degree of mutual respect. One always admires the good performer, even if he belongs to the other side. He excels within precise and well understood rules, which anyone who wishes to play the game at all has to observe. We can illustrate this within the framework of two different sets of rules, those of the House of Commons and those of diplomacy.

Here first of all are three members of Parliament, two Labour and one Conservative, fencing and gently teasing one another, and obviously enjoying themselves. They are performing in a theatre they understand, the play is of no great political importance and they are members of the same company of actors. The debate is on the dependent relatives of single women and the need for the Government to provide tax benefits for them.

Dame Irene Ward I was delighted that the Hon. Member for Halifax made the point that this motion was introduced by a man. Men are very susceptible, if one can get at them. The trouble is, one never can. We can see an example of that today, when there are so few Members here. They rush out because they are terrified of being involved in something which they do not understand. I therefore hope there will be a real result for them from the motion, which I wholeheartedly support, for the National Council for the Single Woman and her Dependants, organised by the Rev. Mary Webster with the support of all parties and all types. There is a growing need in the country today.
Mr. W. A. Wilkins I think that my Hon. Friend the Member for Halifax (Dr. Summerskill) is wrong in her view that because we are males we take no interest in a subject of this kind. This is a quite unfounded allegation. I have been interested in this for many years.
Dr. Summerskill I pointed out that males who do take an interest are unique and rare. My Hon. Friend falls into that category.
Mr. Wilkins It is the first time I have been called unique or rare, but I am delighted to hear it from my Hon. Friend.[19]

This is the Parliamentary game at its most agreeable. Members are one another's Hon. Friends, always refer to one another in the third person and take pleasure in the elegance of a phrase. It is all very different from the crude world outside, in which the frontal attack, spearheaded by 'You', is normal, where there is no Speaker to keep erring Members reminded of the club rules and the intimacy of the debating chamber at the House of Commons is missing. The style of British politicians owes a great deal to the shape and size of the hall in which Parliament carries out its business. German, American and Russian parliamentarians have a different style from the British at least partly because they perform on a bigger and differently shaped stage. At Westminster, the natural roarer, ranter and tub-thumper is forced to discipline himself to fit the surroundings and to learn new speaking tricks and a new form of language. Some find the process of adaptation and conversion more comfortable than others. The man who has come up the Trade Union ladder is likely to have problems, but anyone reared in the traditions of the Oxford and Cambridge Unions takes very easily and naturally to what is required of him. The point to emphasise most strongly in the present context, however, is that the House of Commons discipline, like that of prison and the Army, is no respecter of persons or opinions. All have to conform equally. Having learnt to play the political game the House of Commons way, nobody is quite the same again. Its methods and manners become second nature and to have learnt and absorbed them has an effect not at all unlike attending the same public school. As individuals Members of the House of Commons, or for that matter the House of Lords, may be very different from one another. Opinions may cover a wide range and personal antagonisms may be as marked and as frequent as personal friendships, but the fact of being exposed to the same atmosphere and the same code of conduct month by month and year by year does undoubtedly bind one Member and ex-Member to another, unwelcome as this may be to some. They are brothers in language and brothers in etiquette.

The House of Commons style is a strange mixture of the formal and colloquial, but it reads less colloquially than it sounds, mainly because those responsible for the transcript always print verb and pronoun forms in full. One consequently reads 'it is' and 'who would', instead of 'it's' and 'who'd'. The flavour of a House of Commons speech, as it is preserved for posterity, is consequently misleading. These people are not necessarily as pompous, precise and nineteenth century as they may appear to be.

Suppose we take, for instance, an extract from a debate which took place in 1972 on the Night Assemblies Bill, a subject not calculated to lead to the highest oratorical flights or to bring the Parliamentary heavyweights to their feet, or indeed into the Chamber at all. The two speakers at this point were both in their early forties and both belonged to the Labour Party.

Mr. Golding It is clear that the type of people whom the Secretary of State for the Environment would appoint to such a Committee would be latter-day Inspectors-General. We could

expect the choice to be of people whose attitudes towards life are ones of restriction. Without doubt the type of Committee appointed by the Secretary of State for the Environment would be composed of Establishment figures. It would include Privy Councillors and that sort of thing.
Mr. Kaufman Lord Goodman.
Mr. Golding Yes, indeed, there would be the same old faces, the old, the comfortable, those who have lost all spark and imagination. We would get on such a committee those who think that order consists of a comfortable armchair by a fire, and these would be the wrong people to deal with this question, because by their very nature those who want to assemble in numbers of 5,000 or more in the open air are not the comfortable men and women in armchairs, the old, the wise, those who have given up the struggle in society. The people who want to congregate outside will be anti-Establishment. They will be the long-haired.
Mr. Kaufman Not necessarily.
Mr. Golding They will be bearded, the badly dressed. We know that this committee sitting in comfort in the London boardroom will base its attitudes on an image it has of these people. It will draw up rules, regulations and restrictions, based on an antagonism towards all who would challenge the Establishment. That is one of the fundamental objections to the Bill and that is why I oppose the Clause.[20]

These were not in the first place words printed. They were words spoken in a particular accent, with a particular degree of light and shade, of emphasis and throw-away, of irony or dead-pan, of pomposity or lightness of touch. None of these essential characteristics of the contributions to the debate made by Mr. Golding and Mr. Kaufman is transferred to the printed page, and the consequent misunderstandings can be very great. In what tone of voice did Mr. Kaufman say 'Lord Goodman'? Was it mocking, weary, cheerful, questioning, depressed? How did Mr. Golding actually say 'They will be the long-haired'? In a neutral, matter-of-fact fashion? Despairingly? In inverted commas?

The point is extremely important. How something is said is of at least equal importance to what was said. The effect depends on manner, and the language of politics is not necessarily language as the lexicographer and grammarian understand such matters. If Mr. Golding had happened to have a Glasgow accent or a Birmingham accent, the impression made on his listeners would be quite different from what it would have been if his Eton and Oxford upbringing had been unmistakably reflected in his voice. It is hardly possible for *Hansard* to indicate such niceties, but the student of language is not carrying out his professional duty if he fails to bear them constantly in mind.

If one is equipped only with the printed word, as is usually the case, one has to make deductions and assumptions, and they can well be wrong. In the extract given above, for instance, it makes a great deal of difference to our assessment of his style if he said 'It is clear that the type of people', or 'It's clear that the type of people'; 'those who have lost all spark and imagination', or 'those who've lost all spark and imagination'. To use the first form in spoken English is to deserve the label of pedant, but whether or not Mr. Golding should be thought of in this way it is impossible to say. The evidence is incomplete. But anyone who wishes to test for himself the extent to which it is possible to be grossly unfair to politicians and to write them off unheedingly as pompous asses has only to read Mr. Golding's remarks aloud in the two possible forms, one with the contractions and one without – 'they'll be', not 'they will be', 'that's why', not 'that is why', and so on. Better still, one can compare the effect of a speech as it sounded in the hall or on television with Press reports of the same speech. The difference can be remarkable.

Diplomatic language, which overlaps with political language, is masonic in a different way from Parliamentary language. The essential qualities of diplomatic language have been well explained by Lord Strang. 'Diplomacy,' he writes, 'has a conventionalised vocabulary and turns of expression and ways of thought which are common coin in both tongues (English and French) and indeed in European tongues generally. The things that governments say or write to each other, whether direct or in international organisations, are comprised within what one may call, in the broadest sense, the political sphere, where the subject matter is familiar to all governments. Diplomacy is not one of the more exalted or far-ranging or deep-searching of human activities. It makes no heavy demands upon the capabilities of language.'[21]

The purpose of diplomacy is to achieve what Lord Strang calls 'accommodations or agreements'. Diplomats have discovered, generation by generation, that the most likely way of achieving this is by 'seeking precision, by cultivating rationality rather than emotion, by practising guarded understatement, by avoiding irony, by taking the heat out of controversy, by inspiring confidence'. For this purpose, 'they can draw upon a simple, well-tried and internationally accepted diplomatic vocabulary—words like *détente* or *modus vivendi* – borrowed chiefly from Latin or French. They are also assisted by those mild diplomatic phrases by which governments can, by careful gradation of emphasis, say the plainest things to each other without raising their voices. They "cannot remain indifferent" to this. They view something "with grave concern". They may go further and say that they "will be obliged to consider their own interests", or – and this is a pretty serious thing to say – that they "decline to be responsible for the consequences".'[22]

Ministers, their civil servants and their diplomatic staff share this language together. They are able to take it and the habits of mind which go with it for granted. The general public can hardly be expected to take the same attitude and for this reason any political pronouncement on the subject of foreign affairs is likely to seem lacking in candour and precision, evasive and lacking in real meaning, to be interpreted with the same degree of ingenuity and detective skill as is required to read between the lines of the Russian or Chinese press.

The Foreign Secretary, Secretary of State or Foreign Minister is in a difficult situation in this respect. He is required to be a middleman, with responsibilities both to his diplomatic staff, who would much prefer to tell the general public nothing, and to the electorate, who demand to be told everything. To satisfy both parties is clearly impossible, but the Minister has to do his best, appearing frank and forthcoming, yet being careful to cause the minimum of international friction by any words he may use in public. In Britain his task is probably not quite as difficult as it is in some other countries, since the British are notoriously indifferent to what goes on abroad and uninterested in foreigners. Foreign affairs can therefore be safely ignored for much of the time, in so far as explaining policy to the general public is concerned. Those ministers concerned with domestic matters are likely to have a rougher and more continuous ride.

A Foreign Secretary who is doing his best to be discreet and at the same time not to be infuriatingly vague or fence-sitting will produce something like this, in answer to a television question about his views on the establishment of a Palestinian state.

'We have left the option open, I think rightly, because it is a central part of the negotiations. We are committed to a homeland for the Palestinian people, but not necessarily a sovereign state; that is our position, and we will not toughen that up. We will say this should be subject to negotiation and one of the things on the agenda for Geneva.

'What is necessary, there is no doubt now, is for Israel to give some message to the Arab world that they are serious about territory. If they were to say, for instance, we have no territorial demands, only security needs, it would shift away from the feeling that the Arab world has that the Israelis actually want territory, not just for security but for its own sake, I think that would be very helpful as a background to the detailed negotiations on territory.'[23]

This seems as good a blend of information and tact as one is likely to get from a Foreign Secretary on such an occasion, with Arabs, Jews, and the members of his own Foreign Service all waiting to pounce on the slightest sign of bias or of intention to steer the negotiations in any particular direction. Dr. Owen's professional colleagues would surely have felt that their pupil had done them credit on this occasion. Not all Foreign Secretaries would have learnt the diplomatic approach so well or so quickly.

One Foreign Secretary who never learnt or conformed was Lord George-Brown. As Mr. George Brown, he was the despair of the upper ranks of the Foreign Service, who were greatly relieved to see him go. Temperamentally, he was totally unsuited to the job. He was frequently involved in public scenes and disputes with journalists, press lords, photographers, his ambassadors and even his Prime Minister. When it was pointed out to him that this kind of conduct did the reputation of Britain no good at all, 'Mr. Brown said in so many words that he was what he was and that the country must accept him as such',[24] ignoring the cardinal rule that the Foreign Office is a ministry of diplomats and its chief is, or should be, Britain's first diplomat. 'The Foreign Secretary is the man who creates the image of Britain abroad and not at home, and the manners which may even be a trifle endearing in the hurly-burly of domestic politics are quite out of place in the international arena.'[25] Mr. Brown did not match up to what was required of him. Neither by his words nor his behaviour was he in the least concerned to identify himself either with the professionals in his own Foreign

Service or with the general world of international diplomacy. He had no wish to join them and he proved it by the most unmistakable means known to a politician – he refused to learn the language.

5 Today's Political Abuse

'Abuse', the *Oxford English Dictionary* tells us, is 'injurious speech, reviling, execration'. It suggests a loud, screaming manner, whether in speaking or in writing, and a person driven on by hatred. It is not a pleasant or pretty activity. Its purpose is twofold, to provide an outlet for hostile feelings which can no longer be contained and to expose the object of one's hate to the world as someone deserving scorn, loathing and annihilation.

In an excellent essay, 'The Language of Abuse', David Watt has suggested that the British are not very good at it. 'As a nation,' he says, 'we are notoriously terrified of our own emotions. And in politics we have good reason to be – seeing where political emotion has taken us and others in the past. One rather odd result of this, at any rate in the last century, has been the lack of a really full-blooded vocabulary of disapproval in British politics. We are far outclassed in imaginative invective by the Americans and the Australians.'[1]

This may be true, but is this kind of inferiority something to be ashamed of or proud of? Is a 'full-blooded vocabulary of disapproval' a mark of a highly developed or a culturally backward nation? Mr. Watt does not make his own position in the matter entirely clear. Noting that, among his fellow-countrymen, 'blackguard' and 'ruffian' are unparliamentary and out, he believes that 'we do not trust our political passions and emotions outside their locked cages, and, indeed, as soon as someone comes along with the key that opens them – a poetic gift of the gab or a faculty for heightening our hatred and contempt – we tend to distrust him as a demagogue, even when he is a great man, like Gladstone or Lloyd George. On the whole, this is a safe instinct. But it does make our political language more drab than most.'

Before accepting or rejecting Mr. Watt's analysis, one might usefully ask if he intends his argument to apply to the British population as a whole or only the more educated parts of it. Recent experiences – the Grunwick dispute, the firemen's strike, National Front marches – suggest that the British working class does not keep its political passions in a locked cage. Hatred, contempt and abuse are much to the fore on occasions such as these and the general atmosphere is frequently one of near-savagery. The middle-classes, it is true, strongly disapprove of such goings on, but that is not quite the same thing as saying that 'as a nation we are notoriously terrified of our own emotions'. And why 'notoriously'? It is, perhaps, going a little far to be 'terrified' of one's emotions, but one does well to be cautious of them. To allow free rein to the emotions, something of which Mr. Watt would surely not approve, is to throw away most of the lessons which civilisation should have taught us. Society as we know it could not survive an emotional free-for-all. In any case, which particular emotions or passions does Mr. Watt have in mind? Love? Murderous hatred? Greed? Compassion? Terror? Lust? There is, of course, a school of thought which says that, within the limits of the law, one should make no attempt to keep one's feelings in check. A violent quarrel or a smashing-up of property is psychologically beneficial and all the parties concerned are a great deal better for it. Domestically, this may be so, although such a course of action may turn out to be expensive and that in turn can produce problems as great as the original frustration and inhibition. Politically, however, there is a great deal to be said for keeping matters under control, as diplomats well understand. Putting the point the other way round, what good does political abuse do, except possibly to make the person pouring out the abuse feel better afterwards?

In any case, the law in Britain does not look favourably on unbridled abuse, realising that it is often likely to lead to a breach of the peace. So, as David Watt points out, 'we are always scraping the barrel for ways of being insulting without raising the pulse-rate too much. Mostly we come up with drab grey words like unworthy, improper, despicable and so on. Sometimes, though, we dredge up something more bizarre and flamboyant, like our latest discovery, the word "obscene". I like this usage very much, because it is such a marvellous throwback. Historically speaking, the Labour Party is a creature of non-conformist England; and the whole solid weight of 19th century moral disapproval lies behind its use of "obscene".'

It is worth spending a few moments looking at 'obscene' more carefully. Its history is not quite as David Watt suggests. During the past four centuries there have been two meanings or shades of meaning for it. The *Oxford English Dictionary*, a conservative and moral work, defines them in this way.

1. 'Offensive to the senses, or to taste or refinement; disgusting, repulsive, filthy, foul, abominable, loathsome. Now somewhat arch.'
2. 'Offensive to modesty or decency; expressing or suggesting unchaste or lustful ideas.'

Whether the new popularity of 'obscene', in a political context, derives more from the first or the second of these meanings, it is difficult to say. The one with a continuously strong tradition is the second and it is probably this that David Watt has in mind. The second, it is interesting to observe, was described by the *Oxford English Dictionary* – the editorial work on this particular volume was carried out in the Twenties – as 'now somewhat archaic'. In my own opinion, the present use of 'obscene' as a political word derives quite as much from (1) as from (2). To the Left, wealth is 'obscene'; discrimination against blacks is 'obscene'; the Stock Exchange is 'obscene'; slum housing is 'obscene'; unemployment is 'obscene'. In all these cases, Sense 1, rather than Sense 2, would seem to be the source, although there is undoubtedly, as Mr. Watt suggests, the added implication that such things are morally disgraceful. The word, whatever its pedigree, is certainly immensely powerful nowadays, especially among the young. What is labelled 'obscene' causes a modern person to shudder with horror quite as much as a pair of obscene unclothed female legs did to the Victorians.

Fashions in abuse clearly change. 'Obscene', in its political applications, is no older than the present decade, and the Communist vocabulary of insult and condemnation which aroused George Orwell's despair and anger in 1946 has long since worn itself out and been replaced by words and phrases with a more contemporary flavour. In its day, Orwell's famous quotation from an unfortunately anonymous 'Communist pamphlet' hit the centre of the target. Now it is a period-piece, although still horrifying as an example of the destructive effect that fanaticism can have on language.

All the "best people" from the gentlemen's clubs, and all the frantic Fascist captains, united in common hatred of Socialism and bestial horror of the rising tide of the mass revolutionary movement, have turned to acts of provocation, to foul incendiarism, to medieval legends of poisoned wells, to legalise their own destruction to proletarian organisations, and rouse the agitated petty-bourgeoisie to chauvinistic fervour on behalf of the fight against the revolutionary way out of the crisis.'[2]

As Orwell has pointed out elsewhere, Marxist phraseology consists largely of more or less literal translations from the German or Russian. They may have a meaning in Russian, but they fit very awkwardly indeed into English. 'Lackey' and 'flunkey' are cases in point. 'Pre-revolutionary Russia', notes Orwell, 'was still a feudal country in which hordes of idle men-servants were part of the social set-up; in that context "lackey", as a word of abuse, had a meaning. In England, the social landscape is quite different. Except at public functions, the last time I saw a footman in livery was in 1921. And, in fact, in ordinary speech, the word "flunkey" has been obsolete since the 'nineties, and the word "lackey" for about a century. Yet they and other equally inappropriate words are dug up for pamphleteering purposes. The result is a style of writing that bears the same relation to writing real English as doing a jigsaw puzzle bears to painting a picture. It is just a question of fitting together a number of ready-made pieces. Just talk about hydra-headed jackboots riding roughshod over Blood-stained hyenas and you are right.'[3]

At that time, 1944, Orwell drew up a list of frequently-found Marxist expressions on which he pronounced sentence of death. The list included jackboot, hydra-headed, ride roughshod over, stab in the back, petty-bourgeois, stinking corpse, liquidate, iron heel, blood-stained oppressor, cynical betrayal, lackey, flunkey, mad dog, jackal, hyena and blood-bath. In due course the sentence was carried out and a diligent search of the *Morning Star* and other regular Communist publications in the English language will reveal these once indispensable expressions only very infrequently nowadays. The basic tone is the same—'the need is consciously to link these various struggles into one mainstream against big business domination and for far-reaching social change. Furthermore, in the course of the struggle for the economic and other related social demands, the people will come to recognise the activities of the big monopolies as the root cause of the crisis'[4]—but the new key-words have a more scholarly and, on the whole, more English appearance. The Revolution has become a trifle less aggressive, loud-mouthed and brash, and for that one can only be grateful. Let us look at some of the words which would assuredly cause Orwell to reach for his attacking pen today, if he had lived to continue his crusade into the

Seventies. Set out alphabetically, as a Child's First Glossary of Communist Abuse, they might read like this:

> *banditry* 'attempts by a capitalist country to influence the conduct of affairs in a socialist country'. One can therefore refer to 'overcoming the effects of imperialist banditry in their country.'[5]
>
> *bureaucratic* applied to any institution in a non-socialist country. So, 'the bureaucratic institutions of the EEC'.[6]
>
> *capitalist* a very important and comprehensive Communist term of abuse. It means, broadly speaking, anyone who accepts the capitalist system and who derives an above-average income from it. It is, for all practical purposes, synonymous with the upper middle-class and it is possible to be a capitalist even if one is employed as a salaried manager. A person carrying out exactly the same work in a socialist country is not, of course, a capitalist. The essential feature of a capitalist, as the Left sees him, is that he does little or no useful work himself and lives disgracefully well by exploiting the labour of others. Directors of companies are particularly dangerous and hostile figures and have to be attacked and destroyed 'in the course of developing activity against the capitalists'.[7]
>
> *counter-revolution, counter-revolutionary* attempt, whether successful or not, on the part of a non-socialist party to set up a government, even by entirely legal means. Any person involved in such an attempt is, of course, a counter-revolutionary, someone who is trying to get in the way of the revolution and stop it happening. 'The danger of counter-revolution in Portugal'[8] meant the possibility of a Parliamentary democracy of the Western type coming to power.
>
> *imperialist* the foreign policy of any non-socialist country is always and necessarily imperialist, even though the country in question may have no intention or wish whatever of possessing an empire. 'The right-wing Labour leadership works to maintain capitalist and imperialist policies.'[9]
>
> *liberal* anyone who believes in the desirability of gradual change and is opposed to revolutionary methods. The militant Left, which believes in the necessity of revolution and violence, uses 'liberal' as an expression of contempt and abuse, so that to say a man holds liberal views is no longer to praise him. 'A collection of white, liberal do-gooders.'[10]

middle-class a very nasty insult indeed. Objectively, it means little more than the salary-earning class, but for the Left and a considerable proportion of the young it is a particularly vicious term of contempt, a label for everything that is reactionary, uncreative and despicable. 'The pseudo-revolutionary middle-class totalitarians'.[11]

monopolist, monopoly Any large industrial enterprise in a capitalist country is a monopolist or monopoly. A correspondingly big and powerful manufacturing concern in a socialist country is, for some reason, not a monopoly. 'The monopolists, such as British Leyland, ICI and English Electric.'[12]

reactionary Any non-socialist activity is automatically reactionary. 'A reactionary backlash to legislation on equal pay'.[13] All activities of socialists and communists are necessarily 'progressive'.

so-called bogus, not what it purports to be. Nothing done by capitalists or non-communists is what it purports to be, and it is therefore natural and correct to refer to the British Government's 'so-called diagnosis of Britain's ills',[14] which are obviously and by definition made by a bunch of frauds and incompetents.

wealthy upper middle-class, with strong overtones of hate and jealousy. The 'wealthy' are not necessarily wealthy at all. 'The wealthy have educated their young under the most intensive conditions possible, namely the secluded boarding school.'[15]

In today's political and social conditions, it may be obscene to be a capitalist, middle-class, reactionary or wealthy, but people of this degree of obscenity would probably be permitted to speak at British universities, permitted, that is, by the student body. What would never be allowed, however, would be a meeting addressed by someone known to hold views characterised by extreme obscenity, that is by a public figure who believes that intelligence is an inherited characteristic or that the immigration of coloured people into Britain is dangerous and should be checked. Such people may expect the kind of reception given to the advocates of contraception, pacifism or nudism in Victorian times. They must not be given the opportunity to speak or to propagate their opinions in print. They are in every sense evil and decent citizens have a duty to hound them out of public life by every means at their disposal.

We have more or less disposed of the Victorian obscenities, but the new ones which have taken their place are just as powerful and as pervasive. To be able to show that someone is 'élitist' or 'racist' is to damn him and ruin his career, just as surely as proof of homosexuality did until comparatively recently. Anyone who holds the 'obscene' views of his time, as a great many people undoubtedly do, does well to keep quiet about them. This is not in any way a new situation. For 500 years at least there must have been intelligent, thinking men and women in every generation who found certain aspects of Christian teaching, theology and practice difficult to accept, just as there are people in the Soviet Union and the other Communist countries who cannot, in the privacy of their own mind, swallow the Party line. In such circumstances, the most effective way of destroying an opponent is to prove that he holds forbidden opinions, Communism in the United States, 'racism' in Britain. The most formidable and dangerous insult one can hurl at a man is one, which, if it can be made to stick, will end his career or, at the very least, block his progress.

The technique is well understood by politicians and political organisers in all countries. A classic instance of it was seen in 1932 during the American primary elections. The Depression was at its worst and the poverty and misery of many voters, especially in the rural areas, made them susceptible to any suggestion that the cause of their wretchedness could be pinned down to 'un-American' thinking and practices, to an enemy, in fact. In North Carolina, Robert R. Reynolds defeated Senator Cameron Morrison by a highly effective and disgracefully unscrupulous trick. 'Reynolds would flourish a jar of caviar before rustic audiences and say of Senator Morrison, "Cam eats fish eggs, and Red Russian fish eggs at that, and they cost two dollars. Do you want a Senator who ain't too high and mighty to eat good old North Carolina hen eggs, or don't you?"' [16]

These tactics reached their peak during the McCarthy witch-hunts of the Sixties, when the persecution of anyone believed to have been the mildest socialist sympathies blighted the lives of thousands of American citizens, inside and outside politics. They are still effective. To be accused of being a Red or a Commie does a public figure no good at all. The implication is that he is a potential, if not actual traitor, anti-American and ready to sell his country's secrets at any moment to the highest bidder. The smear does not have as much power in Europe, but it can be inconvenient and most holders of public office would go to some pains to avoid or disprove it.

The whole question is bedevilled by the important issue of what is usually called 'free speech', that is, the right to give public utterance to anything one pleases. The struggle for free, or as it should have been called, freer speech, has been central to political and philosophical activity in both Europe and America since the seventeenth century. By the outbreak of the First World War, speech was probably as free as it had ever been or is ever likely to be, but it would be an illusion to believe that the millenium had been reached. In most Western countries, one could curse and attack one's political opponents in public with something approaching impunity, and that was certainly a great historical triumph. But to attack or ridicule the Christian religion, the monarchy, the judges, or local employers could well bring unpleasant consequences for the offender. To indulge in open criticism of powerful entrenched interests is never a safe or prudent thing to do, no matter how liberal the régime may seem to be.

The most difficult time at which to be active in politics, or indeed at which to be alive at all, is when the shibboleths are changing, when new forms of the unspeakable and unthinkable are developing inside the skin of the old. At such times, people reared in one set of values are faced, first, with the task of understanding that new values are being created and, second, with the unpleasant necessity of accommodating themselves to them. In the process, the old standards of black and white, the old style of humour, the old language of praise and blame are undermined and eventually changed to an extent which older people in particular find bewildering. They no longer know who the heroes and villains are, they cannot follow what is happening on the stage and they are unsure of the moments to cheer and the moments to hiss and boo.

In the Western world, the Sixties and Seventies have been such a time. New devils have been identified, new angels have flown in to confuse us. What was once praiseworthy or at least inoffensive conduct suddenly becomes the act of a bad citizen. The point was admirably made during January 1978 by a celebrated legal case in Britain and by the controversy surrounding it. The facts themselves were simple. Britain, a country which is justifiably proud of its long tradition of free speech, also has a comparatively recent law, which makes it an offence to do or say anything which is likely to stir up racial hatred or dissension. A member of an extreme Right-wing political organisation was accused of having used in public the words 'wogs, niggers and coons' and to have welcomed the death of a black youth, for which he and his organisation were in no way responsible, in terms which suggested that he would not be unhappy to see all the other coloured people expire within a short time. Judge McKinnon acquitted him, saying, in effect, that he was doing no more than exercise his right to free speech, that there was no evidence that he had been inciting anyone to hatred or violence, and that it would be a sad day for Britain when it was no longer possible for a man to say 'wogs, niggers and coons' if he felt like it.

Judge McKinnon then received more abuse than any other British judge has had to face in recent years. He was accused, naturally, of being a racist and there was a widespread and very vocal demand from the Left that he should be removed from his office, a step which the Government did not take, although the Judge was apparently told by the Attorney-General that his attitude was out of date and politically embarrassing and that he would do well to watch his words and his actions more carefully in future.

The case was of great importance in many ways, not least in demonstrating how a new and extremely explosive vocabulary of abuse had developed, without a large and influential section of the population, including the Judge, being aware of the fact. Without any question there are thousands of decent, kindly English people for whom 'wog' and 'nigger' are not strong or offensive words at all, and who are accustomed to using them in a humorous way and completely without malice. Equally, it appears, there are thousands who react to these words much as a respectable Victorian woman would have done if she had been called a whore.

The following letter from an English provincial newspaper[17] illustrates the point. Written by a 'Captain TD' in one of the shires, it begins:

> Every report I have read in the newspapers and heard over the air has had a strong bias towards the opinions of the very small, but voluble minority of people who wish to give the coloured population of this country preference in all things. So far as I can see, there is nothing so special about a black man which warrants this.
>
> For many years Americans have been called by a name to which they do not seem to have objected. Australians refer to us by the name, I believe, of 'Pommies'. I do not mind. We call them 'digger'. I am told that 'Quakers' came by their name through a

peculiarity in the way they worshipped. There are many 'pet' names which are used today, and no offence is taken or intended, so why all the fuss about 'niggers'? After all, nigger is a perfectly good Latin word meaning 'black'.

The race issue is one of the red herrings dragged about by both parties and if the media would give them less publicity they would die a natural death instead of the violent one they are approaching. No law can make one man love another, and the race law of this country is having the opposite effect. If the coloured population would be more tolerant towards the natives of this country, instead of trying to bulldoze its way into everything with the help of its friends, there would be tolerance all round.'

Everything in this letter, viewed objectively, is absolutely true, but it speaks the language of a past age and shows little understanding of the realities of the present political situation. It is quite possible that the next General Election in Britain will be won and lost on the racial issue, so that the leaders of all parties are bound to be extremely sensitive to anything which seems likely to exacerbate it or push it out of control. The damage caused by unrestricted immigration has already been done and Britain, like the United States and France, now has a large coloured population. These immigrants, most of whom, especially the blacks, are working-class and poorly educated, are strongly disliked and feared by a large number of British people, who feel themselves threatened by fellow-citizens they believe to be inferior. In such a situation, it is not unreasonable that certain forms of free speech, of the wogs and coons kind, should be curbed, preferably by self-discipline, but, if that fails, then by legislation.

The Judge McKinnon controversy confirms what should already have been fairly obvious, that freedom of speech cannot be absolute except in an ideal society which has so far not been reached and that the weapons in the arsenal of abuse are constantly changing and being brought up-to-date. To the Captain TD nigger is 'a pet name', but to the niggers themselves it is a foul insult demanding a violent response and an eventual apology. One can be sure that politicians themselves would be extremely careful not to use it, whether they might belong to the Left or the Right.

One does not, of course, have to use crude terms in order to be insulting. One does not have to use words at all. To move one's seat in a train or a bus because a black person has installed himself close by is equally insulting and likely to lead to trouble. But if one restricts one's insults to words, the indirect approach can be equally wounding.

It is interesting and saddening to observe that extremely unpleasant and ill-mannered things can be said about white people which would, quite rightly, give rise to a political storm of the first order if they were directed at coloured people. There are few more vulgar and sickening passages in modern British political literature than the half-page in Colin Brogan's book, *Our New Masters*, where he is analysing the character of certain prominent figures in the Parliamentary Labour Party, as a result of the General Election which brought Mr. Attlee's Government to power.

'Don't be worried about it,' said a prominent journalist. 'Remember these men are *British*. Their instincts are the same as yours or mine. They will know when to stop.'

'British . There is consolation in the word. To be Unbritish is to be extreme, to be rash and brash and theoretical. That is an accusation which could not possibly be levelled against some of the most prominent of the aggressive back-benchers, the Mountain which could be guaranteed not even to produce a mouse: because it is so British.

'Think of Mr. Konni Zilliacus. The very name recalls the root and heart of Lancashire – Gold Flake packets in the Irwell, and Old Trafford soaking in the rain. Who thinks of Cornwall without thinking of Silverman, and there are two of them? Messer and Levy, Orback and Shurmer remind us of Kent and Canterbury, or, at least, of the Forest of Dean. If the name of Weltzman does not bring to mind the Midlands, what does it bring to mind? With Tiffany we remember the men who drained the fens, and Swingler is all that the Wordsworth country means to man and boy. Janner is jannock, or very near it, and Emmanuel Shinwell is Scotland's own.

'There are others whose names are perhaps less racy of the soil, though quite as authentic, but these are enough to show that the Labour members are all as British as they are made, or, at least, as British as you can make them.'[18]

This is Mr. Brogan's polished way of saying that the Parliamentary Labour Party contains more Jews than are good for its health, and that as a result the new Government is going to be influenced and corrupted by sinister foreign ideas. The Trojan Horse is full of dangerous unbritish Communists.

Outspoken anti-Semitism of this kind, whether straight or diluted with anti-communism is fortunately rare in British politics, but when it does occur it excites much less rage and fury than even comparatively mild remarks about black people and their ways. Nowadays in Britain one can insult a Jew and get away with it fairly easily, but even to insinuate that every black man is not necessarily a paragon is to court serious trouble.

Mr. Brogan's style is, of course, rooted in irony and irony, as many able people have found to their cost, is something the British do not take to kindly. It is a dangerous political weapon to use. Only a small section of the intellegentsia will appreciate the flavour and point of a passage like:

> To say, as Mr. Morrison does, that successful Socialism demands drive, self-sacrifice and even economy – to deny the existence of an economic Santa Claus, is to tell the workers that their stockings will be empty unless they fill them themselves. No wonder there is discontent among the men who have spent their lives teaching the public that all they needed to do was to plant the seed of Socialism and then sit back drinking beer while they watched it grow.[19]

It is no accident that Mr. Brogan should attack Jewish Members of Parliament, Mr. Herbert Morrison, as he then was, and the British working-class in the third person. He is talking about them, not to them, much as he might discuss the undesirable habits of dogs or pigs. He finds it interesting to observe their habits, but he has no wish to attempt to communicate with them directly. They are to be dealt with at a distance. One is bound to wonder if the method succeeds. Mr. Brogan hits nail after nail accurately on the head and hard, but what is the point of the exercise? Whose thinking will be changed as a result? Who will be impressed? The British worker is most unlikely to read his book and Mr. Morrison is most unlikely to modify his course of action as a result of anything Mr. Brogan tells him. Those who will read him with sympathy and understanding will be people who share his opinions and who hate and despise the Labour Party as much as he does himself. What his book, *Our New Masters*, contains as a basic message is that the Left cannot be trusted to run the country, that its leading figures are frauds, hypocrites and, in some cases, rogues, and that someone – at this particular moment himself – has a public duty to expose the Labour Government and Labour Party for the bunch of self-seeking incompetents they are. The insults and the accusations are phrased in a way more calculated to please one's friends than to get under the skin of one's enemies, most of whom are unlikely to get the point anyway. More succinctly, *Our New Masters* was written to make its author and his friends feel better, and this, as we have already pointed out, is one of the main purposes of abuse. It lets hate out of the system.

It is in any case a connoisseur's pleasure to watch a fellow connoisseur doing something well, and Mr. Brogan was an adept performer with words. If one is to say 'You are a fool and a scoundrel', one might as well make the point with all possible elegance. This is nowadays considered an aristocratic, 'élitist', attitude, however, and the current market for elegance is neither a large nor a profitable one. It does fortunately still exist in the House of Commons, as a strange survival from the long past days when politics was essentially a pursuit for gentlemen.

Here, for instance, is Mr. Jeremy Thorpe, a great master of the art of carefully polished insults, telling another member that he is a blundering idiot, with no idea of diplomacy or effective tactics: 'This is a valuable debate and I say at the outset that I in no way impugn either the sincerity or the enthusiasm for this cause of my constituency neighbour, the hon. Member for Devon, West. However, I must tell him that I do not believe that, in seeking to achieve what is a common objective between the two of us, he is necessarily going about it the best way.'[20]

And, in the same debate, Mr. Thorpe says to another Member that the proposal he has made contains no sense and is doomed to utter and instant failure: 'The hon. Member for Nottingham, West, has a great knowledge of these matters and one listens to him with respect. My view is that there would have to be some very great reason for doing as the hon. Gentleman suggested.'[21]

Next Mr. Francis Pym informing the Prime Minister that he is a barefaced, unscrupulous liar: 'When the Prime Minister repeats and reasserts, with that bland, disarming smile of his, that, given time, all will be well and that better days are ahead, nobody believes him.'[22]

Still within the disciplining influence of the third person, and lacking Mr. Thorpe's masterly command of the Parliamentary idiom, Mr. Eric Heffer adopts a more forthright approach, which has, even so, a certain style: 'The right hon. Member for Leeds, North-East has given us an old song. The right hon. Gentleman is an old singer. If the Government does not have the vision to solve the problems with which we are faced, and if the right hon. Gentleman represents the vision that would be offered by a Conservative Government, God help the country if ever the Conservatives came to power. The right hon. Gentleman has talked unmitigated rubbish. I have never heard such ideological nonsense from an Opposition spokesman.'[23]

The four people at whom these shafts were aimed should all have got the message that the speaker disagreed with them and had a low opinion of the policy they were putting forward. But the effect of the fourth passage is quite different from that of the first three. Mr. Heffer is treating Sir Keith Joseph as if he came from the moon or from an aboriginal reserve. Mr. Thorpe and Mr. Pym, on the other hand, give the impression of regarding their victims as erring or misinformed brothers, to be treated with compassion and guided towards a more satisfactory understanding of the matter in hand. They have built rather than burnt bridges. Mr. Heffer has not only burnt all the bridges between himself and Sir Keith, but is glaring and shouting across to him on the far bank of the river.

The distinction is an important one. The diplomat is trying all the time to bring the opposing parties together, to persuade them to reach a workable compromise, without necessarily abandoning their original positions. Few, if any, politicians are diplomats in quite this thorough-going sense, but many would like to maintain good relations with the people they criticise, to have a friendly drink with them once the debate or meeting or television programme is over. Some, however, give the appearance of enjoying or even needing perpetual hostility with their political opponents and of using the kind of language which is calculated to make enemies for life.

Many attacks are so unmistakably hostile and even venomous that one cannot imagine the parties ever spending a friendly hour together. How many of us, accused of being a fraud, a cynic and a hypocrite, would find it easy to invite the author of such a speech or article to lunch? Richard Crossman's published diaries have caused at least one reviewer, in a Conservative newspaper,[24] to use these adjectives and to attempt to justify them in considerable detail. Mr. Crossman's diaries are 'full of titillating glimpses of the prosperous, even self-indulgent, lives of Labour Ministers'. Two of these

Ministers, Mrs. Barbara Castle and Mr. Crossman himself, took a secret Mediterranean holiday on Sir Charles Forte's yacht, despite 'a profound conviction that the acquisition and enjoyment of great personal fortunes is morally offensive'.

The question therefore arises, says the reviewer, 'Can Socialism not be true, though professed by frauds and cynics'. To this the answer has to be, 'it cannot, because the cornerstone of Socialism is a deep faith in the wisdom, benevolence, and selflessness of Ministers and their advisers. Socialism is about state control. It is about taking human destinies out of the hands of individuals (who act only in their own selfish interests) and into the hands of the state. The state is above the petty human vanities which account for all the objectionable features of industrial societies.' Mrs. Castle and Mr. Crossman can therefore be called, with complete justification frauds, cynics and hypocrites. They have subscribed publicly to one set of values and beliefs and they have acted privately in a manner which is totally at variance with these values and beliefs. It is therefore reasonable and in the public interest to put them in the *Sunday Telegraph*'s pillory and throw verbal eggs at them or, in the words of the *Oxford English Dictionary*, to subject them to 'injurious speech, reviling, execration', to sustained abuse, in fact.

It is regrettable that, when the abuse forms an integral part of a reasoned onslaught—that the onslaught is the abuse, in fact—the only part of it which is likely to be quoted elsewhere are the words—in this case, fraud, cynic, hypocrite—which summarise the charge. The evidence itself will not, in all probability, be produced for the benefit of other readers, listeners or viewers. During the Sixties, the period of what the journalists called 'abrasiveness' in British politics, Mr. Wilson and Mr. Heath were fond of belabouring one another with invective of the type of 'fatuous deception', 'twisted truth', and 'crawling to the Americans', which were highly quotable, and intended to score a point without any supporting ammunition. If Mr. Wilson shot 'fatuous deception' at Mr. Heath, he was supposed to fall dead without more ado, so accurate was the aim and so powerful the weapon. Their successors are much less given to abrasiveness; the fashion has passed, together with its protagonists.

'Hypocrisy' is a word much beloved of politicians, and for obvious reasons. If an opponent can be shown to have broken his promises or to have said one thing and done another, he is obviously a shifty, untrustworthy fellow, quite unworthy of the confidence of the electorate. Sometimes the accusations and counter-accusations of hypocrisy become a little too complicated and bewildering for the man in the street to follow. A very fine example of this occurred in the House of Commons in 1968, during a debate on a demonstration and riot which had taken place in Grosvenor Square, in London. The Conservative Member for Ilford North, Mr. T. R. Iremonger, praised 'the commendable behaviour of the police' on this occasion, went on to note accusations of unnecessary police brutality and aggressiveness, and went on in this way:

> I am concerned to look a little deeper into the Grosvenor Square incident. I wish to quote a letter which appeared in *The Times* from Mr. Tariq Ali,[25] who describes himself as the Chairman of the March 17th Ad Hoc Committee. He said in *The Times* of 21st March: 'It is interesting to note the hypocritical protestations of Tory and Labour MPs who get upset when a police horse is hurt but who remain silent at the mounting violence in Vietnam. It is this attitude we demonstrate against, in an attempt to break the silence inflicted on this nation by the two major political parties.'
>
> He goes on to threaten that he will carry out even more violent demonstrations in future. The 'hypocritical protestations' about horses certainly had nothing to do with Vietnam, but it is fair to ask what about the hypocritical protests about Vietnam against the Americans, made by people who are basically anti-American, pro-Communist and pro-Vietcong. What about the hypocrisy of any of these demonstrators, when never a single word is printed that lends voice to these demonstrations by them about all the cruelty done elsewhere in the world—the mass-murder of the Watutsi; the public hangings of the entire opposition front bench in the Congo; the imprisonment of the Soviet writers and of Mr. Gerald Brook; the sacking of the British Embassy in Peking; the mass-murders of civilians in Hué.[26]

It will be noticed from this passage that the chief value of 'hypocritical' is to raise the emotional level of the protest, argument or whatever one likes to call it. It can be omitted without influencing the sense. The 'hypocritical protestations of Tory and Labour MPs' means the same as 'the protestations of Tory and Labour MPs', 'the hypocritical protests about Vietnam' means the same as 'the protests about Vietnam'. But the point of both Mr.

Iremonger's speech and Mr. Tariq Ali's letter to *The Times* is that each side is accusing the other of inconsistency, the idea being, presumably, that the perfect man, the only kind fit for popular trust, is wholly of a piece, driving a straight line through life and never deviating an inch from what he believes to be the truth. Anyone who fails to do this can be labelled hypocritical. The argument is an absurd one – the completely consistent person has not yet been born – but it serves a useful political turn to pretend, and possibly to believe, that one's own side is always firmly consistent and that one's opponents are perpetually shifting from one foot to the other.

And not only one's opponents. In a famous essay[27] attacking the leadership of the Conservative Party, Mr. Enoch Powell savaged those who had been his own colleagues for 'the reversal and inversion of their own pledges'. 'Their fumblings and contradictions', he wrote, 'arise from a deeper and less remediable cause than incompetence. Their declarations, however forthright, their calls, however clarion, would always echo hollow in the public ear. Those who run away once will run away twice. Those who turned at the drop of a hat before and abandoned all they had said will do the same again. Those who stuck to office in 1972 though every twist and tergiversation will not behave differently another time. Neither the penitential white sheet nor the cardboard coat of shining armour will now disguise the sort of people who are wearing them or restore the faith of a nation in the words of those who broke them before. It simply will not wash.'

Mr. Powell, who writes as well as he speaks, leaves his readers in no doubt at all that he considers the Conservative front bench to be a bunch of poltroons, contemptible in every way. He is a specialist in reasoned polemic and in this particular article he is on his best form. It is interesting, however, to observe that he never uses the conventional vocabulary of political abuse. The terms 'hypocrite', 'coward', 'liar', 'twister' and 'spineless' do not occur at all in his article, even though he is on this occasion free of the linguistic discipline of the House of Commons. Mr. Powell is not a man to mince his words and, if he keeps clear of the conventional language of abuse, it must be because he finds it vulgar and demeaning or because he believes that the slaughter can be more effectively accomplished with other weapons.

A person who first leaves the political troupe with which he has been performing for years and then denounces them publicly for their sins and shortcomings is unlikely to find himself greatly loved, either by the people he has abandoned, or by journalists, most of whom prefer to see a neat, tidy political line-up, with all the players wearing their proper shirts, so that the commentator knows exactly who is playing the ball at any given moment. Mr. Powell is easily dealt with. He can be labelled a racist, because he is on record as saying that it is a bad thing to have so many black and brown people in Britain, which is traditionally a white country. 'We are,' the Conservative Party can say, 'very glad that he has left us, because, holding views like that, he would be an embarrassment to us'. The fact is always overlooked that, if Mr. Powell is to be written off and buried as a racist, he is at least a very special kind of racist, since the speaks Urdu and has a great knowledge of and affection for the Indian subcontinent, its peoples and its civilisation. It is just that he believes that the right place for Indians is India and the right place for black people is Africa or the West Indies, much as one might feel that tigers and monkeys are more suitably domiciled in their natural habitat than in the London Zoo.

But Mr. Powell is that dreadful creature, to be scorned by all decent people, the 'defector'. 'Defector' is a much-used and very odd term. The basic meaning is clear enough, a person who, of his own free will, leaves one country or organisation to which he owes allegiance and takes up physical and spiritual residence in another. So, Rudolf Nureyev 'defected' from the Soviet Union, and Messrs. Burgess and Maclean 'defected' to the Soviet Union. 'Defect' is not, however, a neutral word. There is always a flavour of treason about it, of going over to the enemy with a bagful of secrets and expertise which will be advantageous to the other side. In practice, one can 'defect' only by crossing a clear-cut practical line. British doctors do not 'defect' to the United States and British machine-tool setters do not 'defect' to Australia. A doctor or an engineer, who for one reason or another became tired of England and transferred his skill to Bulgaria or China, might well be considered to have 'defected'. The defector is not thought of as an honourable person and to call anyone by this name is to abuse him.

Mr. Enoch Powell has been described not infrequently as a defector from the Conservative Party and Mr. Reg Prentice is certainly regarded in the same way by his former colleagues in the Labour Party, for whom his defection to the Conservatives has certainly been as serious and shameful an offence as if he had packed his bags and accepted a flat and a job in Moscow. He has committed the ultimate crime, by deserting 'the workers' and joining 'the bosses' and, in Labour eyes, he was rightly and fairly denounced by Mr. Bob Mellish as 'a nauseating traitor'. Significantly, he has been cursed and abused with particular ferocity by the Labour 'moderates', that is, by the Party's right wing, to which Mr. Prentice himself belonged. Mr. Prentice counter-attacks by saying that the 'moderates' are nothing but a gang of careerists, who would cheerfully murder their grandmothers, if this would make ministerial jobs more likely for them. As one political commentator[28] has written, 'the crime that Mr. Prentice has committed is to make people think', and for this 'he has been given the treatment that the British politicians reserve for defectors', that is, subjected to the crudest possible type of abuse and to Russian-type machinations which are designed to hound him out of political life altogether. The tactics are as subtle as a steamroller and an agile man with his wits about him can see and hear them a long distance away. But their use does not make the British political scene any more agreeable, nor do they help to solve any of the pressing and real problems with which Britain is faced.

It is difficult to decide if ridicule is to be considered a form of abuse. The difference between the two is a subtle one. Abuse usually reaches its victim directly from the front, head-on, whereas ridicule, like its allies, irony and sarcasm, comes at him more obliquely, from the side, round corners and up his trouser legs while he is looking in another direction. One can poke fun from all angles, the intention being, of course, that it is the onlookers who will enjoy themselves, not the victim. If the person who is being made to look absurd is too literal-minded – a familiar failing among politicians, especially of the Left – or insufficiently intelligent or awake to realise what is going on, the pleasure of the spectators is correspondingly increased. The point must not, of course, be made in too subtle a fashion, or nobody will get the reference. For all normal purposes, the following two examples probably contain just about the right degree of wit and sarcasm for safety. Both come from the Report of a Conservative Conference. First: 'Just consider last week's ludicrous scenes in Blackpool. Speaker after speaker strode to the rostrum to deplore Government policy. It is a great word, 'deplore'. It means, 'I am not going to do anything about the problem, but by God I will deplore'. Then, at the end, flanked by Denis Healey, the iron Chancellor with the wooden head, and Jim Callaghan, the past master of masterly inactivity, they all joined hands around the inane totem pole, the Social Contract, and then they tell us that the price we all have to pay for this is worth it for Labour survival.'[29]

And next: 'So out of date are their dogmatic views that instead of having glasses of water on the table at meetings between ministers and the TUC leaders, I am told that they have buckets filled with sand into which heads can be plunged if by some mischance the heresy known as economic reality is ever mentioned.'[30]

This is not, perhaps, politics at its most serious or most constructive, but, as we have suggested earlier, there is something more than a little odd about anyone who takes politics completely seriously. A little playfulness now and again is a great help in maintaining sanity. But, in politics, some people are funny without knowing it and certainly against their will. An instance of this occurred as a sequel to a radio talk by the Duke of Edinburgh.[31] The Duke foresaw that Britain would be leading a 1984-type existence by the end of the century, with individualism stifled and little real personal choice left. Consumer products, he said, would tend towards an average standard, with the gradual elimination of better-quality things.

This brought a furious reaction from Labour MPs, one of whom, Mr. Norman Buchan, answered Prince Philip's last point, by saying, with wonderful and totally unconscious irony, 'It's obvious the Prince knows little of the working classes of this country. He doesn't seem to realise that we are moving towards greater democracy in Britain with workers taking more responsibility in making decisions which affect them personally.' Which was pretty well what the Duke was trying to say. In Britain at least 1984 will be a thoroughly democratic affair. Standards will have been progressively lowered, with a show of hands indicating unanimous agreement at every stage. For those with the courage to laugh, it will all seem very funny.

6 Politicians can be Straightforward, Sometimes

'Inside every politician,' it has been said, 'there is a decent man trying to get out'. A cynic can reply, 'How do you know?', or can correct the statement to read, 'there was a decent man trying to get out, but he stopped trying long ago'. It is unfortunately true that success in politics, like success in business, is rarely achieved, at least nowadays, without doing a good many things which a Victorian would have considered shameful, and rightly so. To lie, evade, tell half-truths, mislead and tread on other people's faces in order to win power *is* shameful and no attempt to rationalise what one is doing by pretending that it is in the interests of the Party, the company or the nation makes any difference. To agree to function month after month as a rubber-stamp to whatever line of action the Party leaders decide is desirable and to anaesthetise one's own opinions and conscience in the process is equally disgraceful. But God has his revenge. A lifetime of corrupt practice shows itself on the face. In modern commerce, industry or politics few successful men escape the unmistakable signs of moral corruption on their face and in their expression. They are not beautiful or noble to look at. The Lord is not mocked.

It is not good for anyone's morale to be regarded by the general public as contemptible. And the plain truth is that, in a great many countries, the man-in-the-street does have this kind of attitude to politicians as a breed. They are, he believes, in the game for power and for what they can get, and the instinct is a sound one. The average modern politician is a poor creature compared with his predecessors of a hundred or even fifty years ago. The notion of an average implies, of course, that some must be above the middle line and some below, and this is indeed so. Every organisation, however bad, East or West of the Iron Curtain, contains a handful of people who are far better than it deserves and who prevent it from rotting and collapsing completely. These sterling characters keep one's faith in humanity alive. But there are also, below the line, a proportion thoroughly twisted and corrupt, not to say evil people who poison the atmosphere and debase the standards of the enterprise. The ranks of politicians – and again one has to say, East and West – contain their fair share of such people, including some who unquestionably are mad, but who continue to hold their jobs down, to the disadvantage of all concerned.

Some, perhaps many politicians see clearly enough what has been happening to society, to the system and to themselves. One such person is the former Labour Member of Parliament, John P. Mackintosh. 'When the House of Commons acquired its great prestige as a legislature in the last century,' he has written,[1] 'MPs supported their leaders and fought over the great political issues, but they also had much greater personal and political independence. They were often relatively secure in their constituencies and their votes in the House had to be obtained by persuasion. At the same time, they demanded and got full accounts of all that the government was doing. Volumes of despatches on sensitive foreign affairs were published as *Command* papers – the House commanded their production – and select committees swarmed all over the very small and inexpensive Whitehall departments'. Nowadays, 'MPs are retained by their constituencies so long as they loyally support their leaders in the House and these leaders treat them with what amounts to contempt'. Among the western democracies, the situation may be particularly bad in Britain – it probably is – but there are elements of it everywhere. It is small wonder that the more responsible, highly educated and influential people show an increasing degree of unwillingness to have anything to do with politics at all. The currency has been debased and its attractions are not what they were.

How then, one may ask, do the people who are professionally active in politics keep relatively sane in these circumstances? Several answers exist. One is to cultivate the split mind, which is roughly what Sir Harold Wilson is supposed to have done during his days as Prime Minister, assuming his account of his own behaviour is reliable. When his day's work was done he simply turned the switch marked 'Politics' to the off-position and either settled down to a detective story or went to a football match or to sleep. Another possibility is the Lenin solution, to live entirely in the world of politics, to accept its values totally and to understand or wish for no other form of existence. And a third way out of the difficulty is to stay in active politics for only a limited time, to do one's stint and then get out before the corruption and damage to the personality becomes total and final.

The Americans have discovered a fourth possibility, which is, briefly, to indulge in an orgy of unscrupulousness, distortion and adulation of the party at election times and then to revert to an extraordinary degree of soberness and quietly logical and independent behaviour until the next bout of election fury comes along. To pass quickly from a volume of *Hansard*, published during the past 10 years or so, to a volume of the *Congressional Record* is a revealing experience. The difference betweeen the two are very great and highly significant. The British House of Commons emerges as a cock-pit, with each party cock taking every opportunity to peck and tear the other. The House of Representatives, by contrast, provides debates in which the participants come across much more as individuals and less as pawns allowing themselves to be moved around the board by the Party's Grand Masters. The *Congressional Record*, both for the House of Representatives and the Senate, has a much more polite, serious and, if the word may be permitted, dignified flavour about it than *Hansard*. Of course Congressmen and Senators represent vested interests, of course they are a constant target for pressure groups of all kinds, of course some of them are offered and accept financial incentives of varying degrees of importance in exchange for following a particular course of action. But they usually do so as individuals, not as mere Party ciphers and, as a result, they contrive to retain a good deal of the status and freedom of action which the British Member of Parliament has lost. It is very difficult for an outsider to make up his mind, on the evidence of the *Congressional Record* alone, as to whether a speaker is a Republican or a Democrat. The reader of *Hansard* has no difficulty. Members of Parliament always wear the Party colours. They are Party men and women first, people second. This is not true to anything like the same extent of the Americans.

There is another very important difference between the politicians of yesterday and today. The modern politician talks far more than his predecessor did, and he gets dreadfully stale as a result. In the nineteenth century politics occupied a relatively small part of a Member of Parliament's day or year; now he is expected to regard himself as a 24-hour a day party man, a salaried professional on constant call. The industrial and commercial executive is in exactly the same position. If he is ambitious or, in some cases, even if he is anxious to survive, he has to reckon to surrender himself body and soul to his employer. There is no essential difference nowadays between Party Man and Company Man. Both are expected to accept the principle of Total Immersion in Work, both protect themselves by means of a thick coat of clichés and formulae, both are exceedingly unwilling to allow their private thoughts and private lives to become the property of journalists and other professionally curious people who are not likely to have scruples about causing them harm, both are flattered to be called professionals, both spend far too much of their day talking to and with people who use exactly the same jargon as they do.

The leader of the British Conservative Party, Mrs. Margaret Thatcher, has described the effect this process can have on anyone continuously exposed to it.

> 'The trouble with politicians is we have to speak more often than we have something to say. And by the time you've been speaking two, three, four or five times a week, while Parliament is sitting, not always in the House, but the many organisations you have to speak to, you feel a bit stale. Now, that's why I always keep some reading going and I always, among other things, I always read some poetry, because the poet has learned to put his ideas into very economical and often very beautiful language. And I find, sometimes, if I read some poetry, that will set you off on a theme. And you must try to find in politics a different approach. There's not much new to say in politics, there hasn't been for years, but it's the approach that's individual and different. There are two themes that I've just been using and must find some more. William Butler Yeats wrote 50 years ago – let me think, can I remember it? "The centre cannot hold. Mere anarchy is loosed upon the world. The best lack all conviction, while the worst are full of passionate intensity." Now you can see its application to a whole number of things. One couldn't have thought up that sort of economy of language to draw on someone else's. Just another one of Kipling's that I will use some time: "Truth is seldom friend in any crowd". This, of course, is obviously the tactic of the demagogue: the presentation rather than the real underlying facts, and you can see the relevance of that to the present situation.'[2]

This kind of personal confession is very refreshing to hear and read. One wonders how many other professional politicians diagnose their spiritual and verbal ailments as carefully and constructively as this, and how many try to discover a remedy. A survey carried out a few years ago[3] revealed that, although British Members of Parliament did not appear to be great readers, such books as did come their way appeared to be about 'political, international or social affairs', which would tend to keep them always in the same mental groove. Mrs. Thatcher's sensible recipe of reading good poetry to renew her sensitivity to words does not, so far as Members of Parliament are willing to disclose such private matters, appear to have been at all widely adopted. But they certainly realise at least part of what is happening to them, and regret it. As the survey puts it:

> Members (particularly newer ones) often openly regret that their parliamentary and other activities seem to prevent them continuing to extend their knowledge. Their life as Members seems to be an infinite series of short-run goals and routine tasks which do not always subside to a manageable level after a Member has 'learned the ropes' of Westminster and gained experience of doing most of a Member's possible tasks (including, even, promoting a private Member's bill) at least once. 'Living off intellectual capital' is the common phrase for this situation: the Member feels so dominated by the techniques of his duties and the flow of events and activities that he has no time to gain new knowledge.[4]

'Living off intellectual capital' is itself, of course, a fairly well-worn cliché, and the fact that politicians instinctively go for it to describe their condition, is itself a symptom of what is happening to them. What they are suffering from and what their chosen career as imposed upon them is not, as they appear to believe, merely a shortage of new infromation and acquaintance with other people's assessments of current affairs, but of sensitivity to words and to the feelings of non-political people. Their lives, like those of Company Men, are desperately short of poetry, humour and balance. Their world, quite possibly against their will, is narrow, bigoted and absurdly inbred. Margaret Thatcher is absolutely right to go for good poetry as an antidote and a stimulus. If more British politicians did the same public life would be great deal sweeter and more worthwhile.

Politics is an essentially urban pursuit and the temptation to escape to one's farm, ranch or country house is as great now as it was in Roman times. There one is free to be onself, to shake off all the cares of Party, State and constituency and to live the life of a happy, innocent human being once again, or so the theory and the fantasy go. It is interesting, therefore, to see how politicians talk about themselves as country creatures. Here is the former Prime Minister, James Callaghan, on the subject of his farm:

> Although, you know, you read all sorts of stories, usually written by malicious newspaper correspondents, about my vast farm and the amount it cost me, and how I borrowed it all at favourable rates. In fact, it was a very straightforward transaction. The money I got from selling my house in Blackheath went into the farm and I borrowed the rest from the Agricultural Mortgage Corporation. And it was really, by present-day standards, because of the inflation that's happened, it was really rather cheap.[5]

Farmer Callaghan goes to great pains to make clear that he is no wealthy landowner:

> I'm losing money, I must say. Let me give you an example. I told Fred Peart this. When I sold some beef a year ago, in April 1973, I got £141 a head. This year I sold the same quantity of beef and got £114 a head, and meantime my fertiliser, my feeding costs, everything has gone up in price, so I want to put over this commercial now. I've lost money on beef this year. Now, Fred knows this and I believe he's responded to it already, and said he's going to do something about it, God bless him.

This, one feels, is not quite private or away-from-it-all enough. Mr. Callaghan, like other leading personalities in the Labour Party, has been accused on more than one occasion of living it up at the public expense, of following a Conservative life-style on the Labour ticket. Here is his opportunity to set the record straight, to show that, by producing beef at a loss, he is in fact subsidising the figure that all politicians are so fond of invoking, wooing and placating, the housewife. 'Fred' is the Minister of Agriculture and the whole passage is too cosy and calculated to take it at its face value. It is not convincing and, for that reason, has to be written off as a political failure, a piece of P.R. that failed to work. Honest Jim has not quite made it.

How, then, does one rate the former Foreign Secretary, Dr. David Owen, on the basis of the following personal statement:

> I like my home – my territory really matters to me. And I believe it is a deep, instinctive drive in all of us, this territorial drive.... It is one of the reasons I encourage people in my constituency to try to have their own territory, buy their house if they can, to make them feel that their house is something which they have some influence on, control of. I am a great decentraliser. I think one of the most dangerous things about some present-day socialist thought is that people want large organisations, bureaucracies. I loathe bureaucracies. I think bureaucracies are deeply against my philosophy as a socialist. But I also think there is something all-embracing about them. I loathe the way we make decisions by committees these days. We do not give individual responsibility enough to people. I prefer people to make mistakes and I would like people to chance their arm. It is a spirit that we have lost in this country-entrepreneurial. Everybody is so damn cautious.[6]

This, one might well say, is good, sound, Conservative, property-owning stuff. Or is it simply human and honest? Why should one not give Dr. Owen the benefit of the doubt and agree that on this occasion, when he is not wearing his uniform as a Labour Member of Parliament or a Foreign Secretary, he has broken through the normal restraints and pretences and is saying what he actually thinks and means? One would certainly like to feel that deep down inside a loyal Party man like this there really was a real person, moved by the same kind of considerations that are important to the majority of his fellow-citizens. But, to anyone of the Left, it could appear dangerously heretical—anti-bureaucratic, pro-entrepreneurial, pro-individual responsibility, pro-owner occupier, anti-large organisation – everything that the Soviet Union disapproves of, plays down or denounces. One needs, of course, to see the face and hear the voice as the words are spoken, but on the evidence of the transcript, one is convinced. This sounds like an honest man, talking with his heart as well as with his head.

When it comes to plain speaking, the old and retired do not, of course, have the same problems as the young and active. Ambition is over, enmities and jealousies have cooled and the events in which one took a leading part are long ago and no longer require secrecy and diplomacy. It is largely for this reason that the memoirs and reminiscences of elderly politicians so frequently made much more agreeable and interesting reading those of men who are still in the fray, or who have only just withdrawn from the thick of it.

Here, for instance, is the former Foreign Secretary and Prime Minister, Sir Anthony Eden, later the Earl of Avon, thinking back to the early days of the Second World War, when Britain was facing a very serious situation and military collapse seemed not improbable.

> There didn't seem to be any means by which we could carry on for more than a few months, once the French collapsed; except, of course, for the anti-tank ditch, the Channel. They were grim days. I remember, for instance, one cabinet meeting; the news coming in was bad and worse, and Winston suddenly said to me across the table: 'About time No.17 turned up, isn't it?' The cabinet looked a little puzzled. And I grinned back, and I said: 'More than time.' The story was that, before the war, when I'd resigned from Chamberlian's government and I was in the South of France, so was he, and we met one night at a roulette table. He said: 'What are you doing?' I said: 'I'm backing No.17', and he said: 'I'll join you.' Nothing happened for a while. Then No.17 turned up. And we left our stakes and it turned up again. So then we took them away, more than satisfied. And that was the reference, but it was very, very grim.[7]

It had all happened thirty-five years ago, and it rings true. This, one feels, is exactly as it was. Sir Anthony and Sir Winston behaved and talked in just this way. The story is well told, without pretence and without frills, by an old man who no longer had power or public responsibility and who, apart from a natural wish to be kind to his friends, was under no obligation to hold his tongue or measure his words. The difference between this Eden and the Eden of the Thirties and Forties was remarkable. As one of his biographers has written:

> Everything fell into the lap of this handsome, gifted young member of what seemed a divinely appointed ruling class. Consorting only with his peers, he found it difficult to grasp the

significance of socialism even though Labour came to power. Imagination was never a strong point of Eden's. As a result his efforts to get across to the poorer people tended to sound either stuffy or condescending. He often referred jocularly to his ignorance of economic affairs and he was unable to remedy this. He had none of the knockabout common sense that could make his contemporary Macmillan a first-class Minister of Housing or Chandos an excellent President of the Board of Trade, and both of them successful businessmen.[8]

What this means, so far as Eden's public utterances were concerned, is that, like anybody else, he spoke best on subjects that he knew a good deal about and badly on subjects that were outside his range and experience. In telling the story about No.17, quoted above, he was not required to stray into unknown territory. He had been present in the casino in the South of France and in the Cabinet Room and he simply recalled, without embroidery, affectation or feeling of inferiority or half-knowledge, what had taken place. It is all very direct and straightforward and nobody should have any difficulty in believing it. The lesson is an obvious one, but some interviewers appear to find it difficult to learn. Ask a carpenter to talk about his work and one will most probably receive a sensible reply. Ask him about the best way to peace in the Middle East or about the Green Pound, and one is unlikely to get a particularly clear or worthwhile answer. He may dogmatise, air his prejudices or produce impressive words which he judges suitable to the occasion, but it is highly improbable that he will rise to the level that he reached when he was discussing the new door he was in the process of fitting. Similarly, Eden on the subject of casinos and Churchill is worth listening to, but Eden on socialism or old age pensions is not.

When he was talking about his farm and his bullocks, in the passage quoted above, the Right Honourable James Callaghan, Leader of the Labour Party and Prime Minister of Great Britain, was speaking as rather more than half a politician and as rather less than half a farmer. Farming is not his trade, he does not do the day-to-day work himself, and he does not depend on it for a living. When discussing farming, he is almost certainly more knowledgeable than the average carpenter is when giving his views on the prospects facing the Middle East, but the essential dimension of professionalism and complete involvement is missing. It is this, together with the in-reference to Fred, the Minister of Agriculture, which causes the interview to strike a false note. Dr. Owen, on the other hand, knows at least as much about buying, improving and running a house as he does about foreign affairs. He is directly concerned with both and he is worth listening to on both, although he is not likely to be as forthcoming and guileless on the second subject as on the first.

If a politician is unable to summon up easy, colloquial language for a press conference or for a radio or television interview, one can be reasonably sure that the habits of caution and formality have become ineradicably fixed in his bones. Dean Rusk served two Presidents as Secretary of State and consequently had a good deal to reminisce about. He was able to do so very pleasantly, keeping his listeners with him all the way:

> Kennedy had informal methods, but President Johnson, if he were concerned about a particular point, would call me instead of some junior officer in the department, and it was much easier to delegate responsibility under him. President Johnson was a very hard task-master. He was hardest of all on himself, and therefore the rest of us lived with it with comfort. I had the impression that he was a man in a great hurry, perhaps he never knew, from one day to the next, whether he would still be alive. He had that massive heart attack back in the 1950s, you see. We could never break him of staying up to one or two o'clock with his evening reading and then getting up at five in the morning to go down to the operations room to check on the casualties from Vietnam. He drove himself mercilessly and, therefore, he drove the rest of us pretty hard.[9]

The information is interesting in itself and was almost certainly new to most of the people who saw and heard Dean Rusk on television. Rusk does not give the impression of holding anything back, or of giving the truth a twist, to suit some special purpose of his own. But everything is safely in the past tense. The two Presidents were safely dead when the former Secretary of State was thinking back for the benefit of his television audience and there were no reasons of State security to prevent these particular disclosures from being made. At the time when these events took place it is most unlikely that Mr. Rusk or anyone else would have offered the public revelations of this kind. One has to wait until leading public figures are off the stage before discovering the most interesting and significant things about them. So long as these great men are still actively engaged in performing their vital public duties, their civil servants and public relations officers will do their utmost to make sure, usually successfully, that only the most favourable and least dangerous versions of events and personalities are presented to the outside world. Later, normally after their death, facts come to light which would almost certainly have changed their reputation and possibly effectiveness considerably, mostly for the worse, had such details been generally known during their lifetime. One thinks, for instance, of what is now known about the amorous habits of President Franklin D. Roosevelt and President John F. Kennedy; the true cultural interests, especially in the matter of music, of John F. Kennedy and his wife; of the acquisitiveness and spendthrift habits of Jacqueline Kennedy; of the corrupt organisation which President Nixon allowed to grow up around the Presidency; of the influence of the courtiers surrounding Harold Wilson; of the selfishness, petulance and vanity of Winston Churchill, and many of the other less than flattering pieces of information about members of the political élite which are kept concealed from the general view until all danger has passed.

But the truth usually does come out, sometimes as a result of jealousy and enmity, sometimes because old people are naturally garrulous and careless of what they say, sometimes as the consequence of painstaking detective work by scholars and journalists, but most frequently by sheer accident. No system of concealment is absolutely foolproof, some people have surprisingly long memories and others have a great many enemies.

One man whose political behaviour in the 1920s and 1930s caused much dissension and anger in the Labour Party was Ramsay MacDonald. He was held by many members of the Party to have betrayed his Socialist principles by deciding to form a coalition government with the Conservatives. Most of his critics accused him of doing this solely in order to remain Prime Minister and to hold on to power at all costs. In 1967 the veteran Labour politician, Emanuel Shinwell, explained in the course of a television interview how the decision affected him personally.

> He asked the second eleven of the government, and I was one of them, to come to Downing Street, when he explained his position. I remember sitting opposite him and telling him that there was no need to do this, and he was furious with me—all the more furious,

because I was one of his intimates. 'What can I do?' he said. I said, 'You can remain as Leader of the Opposition, and let the other side carry on; let them find a way out of the economic difficulties.' He wasn't going to have that. 'Impossible', he said.'[10]

This is good, clean stuff, and it has the ring of truth about it, although with old people one never knows. They have the disconcerting habit of inventing their own version of what happened and then, by rehearsing it over and over again until they are word-perfect, coming to believe implicitly in the truth of what is in fact a wholly fictitious account of what took place. By then all the other characters in the story are dead, cross-checking is impossible and the myth becomes history. But it can be so splendidly and convincingly presented that everyone who hears it is completely taken in and even grateful for such a refreshingly forceful and detailed eye-witness account of an episode which had previously been either unknown or found puzzling.

This caution is not intended, however, to undermine the general validity of the conclusion advanced earlier, which may be rephrased in the form of Hudson's Second Law of Politics, which says that of any two statements made by politicians, that by the old and long retired, who has nothing to lose by frankness and honesty, is usually to be preferred to that by the young and active, for whom the truth can be perilous.

The appearance of frankness and honesty is not, of course, to be confused with the genuine article. One should be especially wary of politicians who make a point of telling the public that they are being frank. This is a sure sign of a cover-up. Sir Harold Wilson was much given to using this word, in this kind of context: 'We have been very frank with the country, and I believe that is true of all parties'.[11]

No party is ever 'frank with the country'. Politics is not like that. But supposing that in this particular context Sir Harold had happened to be making an accurate statement — there was no way of either proving or disproving it at the time — one could be pardoned for suspecting that on most other occasions he has not been frank at all. If frankness is his ordinary custom, as one might possibly have thought it should be, why trouble to emphasise the fact?

Sir Harold was a great master of the art of pseudo-intimacy, which could easily persuade those off their guard that they were being taken into his confidence, talked to man to man across the table. This was the method, illustrated by part of a broadcast discussion with the BBC's leading politician-tamer, Robin Day.

> *Day* Did the Commonwealth Prime Ministers' Conference achieve anything useful?
> *Prime Minister* I think it did. Old stagers feel it was the best Commonwealth Conference we've ever had.
> *Day* Don't you feel that a lot of people here in this country feel that at these conferences Britain appears to be the whipping body of the black Commonwealth?
> *Prime Minister* She didn't get any whipping this time. I admit the Conference in September 1966 was pretty tough. I sat there and took it for six or seven days and then I hit back.[12]

One should note here the clever use which Sir Harold makes of the word 'I'. He was much given to personalising politics in this way, partly to intensify the feeling of 'frankness' and partly to give the impression that he always held the tiller of government. The language is disarmingly colloquial – 'old stagers'; 'pretty tough'; 'I sat there and took it'; 'then I hit back' – and it completely obscures the fact that the Conference to which Sir Harold is referring was a useless, sterile brawl, with blacks throwing bricks at whites and whites unable to make up their minds as to whether to dodge the missiles or throw them back. There is neither simplicity nor straightforwardness in Sir Harold's remarks, merely the illusion of these things. Nothing is precise, there are no facts or details to hang on to, and we are offered only cosy generalisations, put across with a smile and a puff on the pipe, the pipe being used in the Baldwin fashion to guarantee the Prime Minister's honesty and Britishness.

Here, to illustrate the point by contrast is something quite different from the other side of the Atlantic. Senator Dodd was reflecting on the lack of success of his Bill to control what he called 'the flourishing mail order firearms trade'. This Bill had not had the support from the Senate that he felt it deserved.

> The documented research on the need for the legislation was ridiculed as 'inadequate and inconclusive'. Editors of sports magazines, editors who knew better, told their readers the sole aim of the law was to disarm legitimate sportsmen. All this was particularly disappointing to me in view of the fact that just a matter of days prior to the introduction of the original mail order gun bill we concluded a productive series of meetings with

representatives of the firearm industry, representatives of sports organisations, editors, writers, collectors and the National Rifle Association. I was confident in my mind that we had their support for the legislation that would help to disarm the criminal, but at the same time in no way interfere with shooting sports. I was confident that we had a common interest in curbing the ever-growing number of gun crimes being committed each year and on the runway number of guns or descriptions, including military ordinance, then finding its way into the hands of of killers, robbers, teenagers, political extremists and the insane. I believed that as men of goodwill we could find common ground in our mutuality of purpose to pass a law that was in the common interest and that the public was clearly demanding and that would protect the sportsman's interests. I was wrong. We could not count on the gun industry, nor the sportsmen's groups, nor the editors, nor the antique gun collectors, nor the conservationists. After the gun lobby had finished working over the officers of these assorted organisations, most of whom do not seek the advice of their members in formulating policy, they all spoke with the same tongue. As a group the officers of these organisations misrepresented the feelings of millions of legitimate sportsmen by parroting the mouthings of the gunrunners. It was impossible to tell the conservationist from the gunrunner, the legitimate hunter from the paid lobbyist. I did not know five years ago that a group of firearms manufacturers and related businesses formed a National Shooting Sports Federation with the specific purpose of opposing firearms laws, and oppose firearms laws it did.[13]

If Sir Harold Wilson had chosen to discuss the abortive Commonwealth Prime Ministers' Conference in these terms – it would not have been at all difficult – the public would have been given some information worth having. Senator Dodd is putting on record an honest, factual account of what happened. His arguments are clearly stated and easy to follow. He is talking seriously and expects his remarks to be taken seriously, both by the Senate and by the public. Sir Harold Wilson, at least on the occasion to which we have referred above, is not in the same league.

But the sad truth is that, whatever the case may have been half a century ago, the Mother of Parliaments in London is no longer a place where most Members take their tasks seriously enough to make plain, non-party announcements of any consequence. Odd bits of information are passed across from official sources, but they are all too likely to be purveyed in an infuriatingly party-political manner, as in this statement by the Joint Parliamentary Secretary of the Ministry of Housing and Local Government, Mr. James McCall.

> I did not myself check the hon. Gentleman's figures but my hon. Friend the Member for Croydon South was a little more cautious before he entered into this sort of discussion, and took the trouble by means of a question to obtain the figures of what was happening in London. Under the Tory Act Croydon was paid nothing and Harrow was paid nothing. Under our Act Croydon is getting £130,000 and Harrow is getting £88,500. This is clear evidence of the effectiveness of our scheme. Again, what was the position under the Tory Government – did the Tory Government pay 75 per cent of nil? No, they paid 50 per cent of nil. Either the hon. Gentleman's complaint is that nobody ever thought that the Tory scheme would work or produce any money and therefore that was the reason why it had a low grant of 50 per cent, or it is irresponsible to criticise us, who have produced a very much more effective scheme. It is not perfect, but it is a scheme that is producing results, paying half as much again as a proportion of the figures.[14]

One does not expect every Member of Parliament or every Congressman to hold the same views, nor is it reasonable to believe that party allegiances make no difference to a person's way of thinking about certain problems, and quite possibly about life in general. But, when the need to score party points on every occasion and at all costs makes it impossible for a man to talk sense or make a plain statement, something must have gone seriously wrong. The idiotic interweaving of prejudice with facts in the passage by Mr. McCall quoted above is both depressing and funny, according to one's mood. The public outpourings of leaders in the Socialist countries have a very similar effect on anyone reared in the Western tradition, or, at least, what used to be the Western tradition.

It is a great pity that the world outside the United States obtains its picture of political life in that country from the corruption-scandals which blow up from time to time, as they do anywhere and from the buffoonery, bribery and circus-tactics which tend to characterise American elections. These warts and blemishes on the American skin, so beloved by the world's journalists, conceal the fact that under that skin is a remarkably effective political system, which is democratic in the best sense, that is, one in which the elected representatives of the people feel free to speak their mind bluntly on subjects which are important to them and on which they take good care to be well informed. At their best – and it would be unreasonable to expect even the most intelligent and most distinguished politicians to be always at their best – the members of both houses of Congress are unsurpassed in presenting an important issue clearly and in a responsible, non-partisan way.

As an example of this and a model of how the job can and should be done, one might take part of a debate on the rights and wrongs of telephone-tapping or, as the Americans call it, wire-tapping. Having referred to wire-tapping, bugging and similar habits in plain terms as 'this dirty business', Senator Brewster addressed the Senate in the following terms:

> The right to privacy is indeed the most comprehensive of all rights. A society which cherishes liberty and human dignity cannot do without it. A society which seeks to abolish individual freedom cannot tolerate privacy. I have always thought that this was what distinguished us from a totalitarian government and yet I see us moving in that direction. A client who talks to his lawyer in confidence is now often talking 'for the record'. The bug may be in the stapler on the desk, in the chandelier or in an inkwell, even in that ludicrous Martini olive. The receiving set may be down the street a block or two. The Government conference room may contain a two-way mirror, and everything said by a client to his lawyer may be audited. The men dressed as telephone mechanics who drive up in a 'telephone' truck may be Government men placing a tap. As one views the increasing intrusions into the various realms of privacy, he is bound to agree that we are approaching what Orwell described in *Ninteen Eighty-Four*: 'You had to live, did live, from habit that became instinct in the assumption that every sound you made was overheard.' We are not yet at that point, but the pattern of surveillance and conformity that possesses us marks gravitation towards it. Electronics have made it easy to penetrate any sanctuary and to break down the walls that have guarded people's confidences. The climate of privacy envisioned by our Founders once allowed

the genius of our people to flourish. I rebel against the loss of that climate.'[15]

Taking the opposite view, Senator Tower said:

Wire-tapping can be an effective device in the fight against organised crime and we must make it available to our crime control agencies if we are truly to deter crime. All our talking against crime is not going to materially improve the situation, and neither is the expenditure of vast sums of money, if we are going to continue to tie the hands of our law enforcement agencies in the vital areas. We must take the offensive against the criminal elements in our society who are daily destroying everything our nation is trying to build. For example, it has been estimated every week organised crime takes more out of the poor communities in this nation throuh the numbers racket than the Federal Government will spend there in a year. If we could seriously hamper this operation there would be more money left in the hands of the poor and consequently less poverty. Of all the things we can possibly do to further the fight against poverty a serious assault on organised crime would be one of the greates steps forward. However, in order to make this assault we must have the necessary tools to carry it out. We must allow wire-tapping under these closely supervised procedures in order that the assault against the mob may begin in earnest.[16]

There is no gratuitous introduction of 'Republican' and 'Democrat' into every other sentence. The two Senators feel big enough to stand on their own feet, and although they may personify the pro and anti tapping groups, they appear before the Senate and the public as individuals with opinions of their own. The results are evident in the language they use. The mouthpieces of committees and parties inevitably talk woolly rubbish. Only the unshackled individual has any chance of talking straightforward sense.

But, running the risk of puncturing the pro-American euphoria which may have built up during the past few pages, it is only fair to say that American politicians are capable of producing some very unattractive thoughts and phrases at times when they believe the world is not watching or listening, and occasionally, even, when the world is tuned in. There have been few more unpleasant and indeed shameful items of political literature anywhere at any time than the records of the witch-hunting operations of the Senate subcommittee under the chairmanship of the late Senator McCarthy, and the transcripts of the taped conversations betweeen President Nixon and his accomplices at the time of the Watergate conspiracy. These are the unacceptable face of rugged individualism in politics, but they do not, fortunately, represent the American norm. The exchanges reproduced below may be vigorous and informal but they are certainly not praiseworthy. Whether they are preferable to the sterile Labour versus Tory stuff of today's House of Commons must be a matter of opinion.

Here is Senator McCarthy in full cry. The subject is Communist infiltration in the U.S. Army and the person being grilled is Brigadier-General Ralph Zwicker. The Senator, with his unpleasant bullying manner, is concerned here with the reason for the appointment of a particular army officer, whose political background, in the Senator's opinion, contained certain dangerous features.

Chairman   General, you understand my question?
General Zwicker   Maybe not.
Chairman   And you are going to answer it.
General Zwicker   Repeat it.
Chairman   The reporter will repeat it.
General Zwicker   That is not a question I mean to decide, Senator.
Chairman   You are ordered to answer it, General. You are an employee of the people.
General Zwicker   Yes, Sir.
Chairman   You have a rather important job. I want to know how you feel about getting rid of Communists.
General Zwicker   I am all for it.
Chairman   Alright, you will answer that question unless you take the Fifth Amendment. I do not care how long we stay here. You are going to answer it.
General Zwicker   Do you mean how I feel towards Communists?
Chairman   I mean exactly what I asked you, General, nothing else. Anyone with the brains of a five-year-old child could understand that question. The reporter will read it to you as often as you need to hear it, so that you can answer it and then you will answer it.[17]

Like most other official transcripts, those made of Senate proceedings are 'verbatim', but one has to define 'verbatim'. What the term means is that the words reproduced are indeed the words spoken, but that there has been no attempt made to transcribe and retain the grunts, pauses, winding-up noises, stumblings and false beginnings which, to one degree or another, characterise all human speech. What is printed is a cleaned-up and improved, but not falsified version of what would have been heard by anyone actually present in the room.

The transcripts of the Nixon tapes, on the other hand, were made for legal purposes and, subject to the limitation of audibility, omit nothing. For this reason they are very unflattering to the speakers, showing them as men unable to shape their thoughts and to express themselves logically. They mumble and they mutter, they begin and then forget what they were intending to say, they use the crudest and most un-public expressions. This, one says, is how politicians really are when the doors are shut and there is no-one, except, as it happened on this occasion, a microphone, to overhear. How many other high-level political discussions in America and elsewhere are like this, one wonders, when the limelight is removed from the stage? Is this really what goes on, is the man inside perhaps even worse than the man outside? Since tapes like these are necessarily rare and since there is no other way of making a total record of this kind, we cannot judge how typical they are, but other sources of information suggest that some private political conversations at least are on a level which would do the people concerned small credit if they were to become more widely known.

President Well, put it this way, put it this way, you draft what you, what you want. And we can, uh, if I have any concerns about it, I'll give you a ring. You can, uh, be around, and so forth.
Dean Uh huh.
President And, uh, but, but, you would agree you should—but nothing should be put out now. Right?
Dean I would agree. I was, I was thinking about that.
President You see, we've got the problem—today the thing may break. You know, with Magruder, uh, and so forth. And, uh, I'm, uh, I—you know what I mean. That's what I wanted to run over with you, briefly, as to, you know, to get your feeling again as to how we handle it, how we—You know, you, you were saying the President should stay ahe—, one step ahead of this thing. Well,

we've got, uh—The point is, the only problem is what the hell can I say publicly? Now, here's what we've done.
Dean Well, you see—
President I called in—I got in Kleindienst. Uh, we're—I've been working on it all week.
Dean Right.
President Actually, I mean I got, as soon as I got the Magruder thing, then I, I got in Kleindienst, and, uh, then at four o'clock we got in, uh, sold uh, Petersen. Kleindienst withdrew, uh, and, uh, uh, assigned Petersen. I said, 'All right, Henry, I don't want to talk to Kleindienst anymore about this case. I'm just going to talk to you.'
Dean Uh huh.
President 'You're in charge. You follow through and you're going through to get to the bottom of this thing and I am going to let the chips fall where they may.' And we covered that all the way down the line. Now, I have to follow him to a certain extent on the prosecution side. On the other hand, on the PR side, I sure as hell am not going to let the Justice Department step out there.
Dean Right.
President and say, 'Look, we dragged the White House in here.' I've got to step out and do it, John.
Dean That's right.
President Don't you agree?
Dean That's right. Uh—
President But yet, I don't want to walk out and say, 'I—Look, John Dean's resignation has been accepted.' Jesus Christ, that isn't fair.[18]

Like two lovers, President Nixon and Mr. Dean understand one another so well that they hardly need words at all in order to achieve perfect communication. But, if this is simplicity, one would perhaps prefer formality and artificiality, always assuming that this kind of person has to be in public life at all.

7 The Real Man Behind the Speechwriters[1]

As we have seen in the previous chapter, most, but not all, politicians appear to have, if not exactly a split personality, at least two quite different ways of expressing themselves, one for occasions which their instincts tell them are safe and another for moments when the enemy is judged to be lying in wait, ready to pounce on the unguarded word and carry it off in triumph. Businessmen display exactly the same characteristics. Their main concern is to avoid saying anything definite or precise in public, in the belief that, in order to survive, one has to surround oneself with a thick, impenetrable layer of vagueness. A thick layer of silence is sometimes used for the same purpose. Both the vagueness and the silence are liable to drive journalists and interviewers mad. There is nothing to get a firm grip on, nothing to argue about, nothing to disagree with.

Edward Heath is a case in point. One of his biographers believes that he 'protects his personality and his inner thoughts by two types of defence. One is the deep moat of silence. The other is the high wall of trite and stereotyped phrases.'[2] There are bound to be those who feel the moat is not worth bridging and the wall not worth climbing. The man inside would be no more interesting than the man outside. Here, they say, is the ultimate, totally formed *homo politicus*, a person with no private life to conceal, a Lenin. The clichés are the man, his blood and bones as well as his skin, so why bother to look below the surface? He is politics on two legs.

To this one may be inclined to make two comments. The first is that Heath, unlike Lenin, does in fact have a number of strong interests outside politics. Music, food and drink, and sailing happen to be three of them. The second is that one does not develop a defence mechanism unless one feels there is something important to defend. In Heath's case, that something appears to be partly political and professional – he has no wish to provide his opponents with potential ammunition – and partly entirely personal – he is understandably weary of accusations that he is cold and unmarriageable. So he prefers to keep his warmth, expansiveness and spontaneous remarks behind armour-plate, and in reserve, for the small circle of friends who can be trusted to understand and appreciate them.

The what-are-you-really-like-Prime Minister question was developed by Leslie Smith, in a broadcast interview with the Prime Minister in September 1969.

> *Smith* You often give the impression externally of being very tough, often pugnacious, yet some of your contemporaries in university days seem to remember you as a very gentle person and they wonder whether perhaps this toughness is as real as you may want it to seem?
> *Heath* I can assure you that I never go around putting on toughness. I don't think that people who do difficult things, and carry through policies which are sometimes controversial because they believe them to be right, are the people who go round saying, 'look how tough I am'.
> *Smith* You seem to be quite passionate, but you very, very rarely show any signs of sentiment. Is this because you think it shouldn't enter politics?
> *Heath* It's certainly not because I don't believe in sentiment, but I'm strongly opposed to being sentimental.
> *Smith* Are you sentimental yourself in any respect?
> *Heath* From time to time, yes. But when one's talking about public life or politics, then I distrust people who try to achieve their ends by being sentimental. On the other hand, sentiment in the sense of deep feeling about various things, life isn't really anything without that. Feeling for the country, or for the sea and the cliffs. I have a deep attachment to my own personal things. I loathe parting with books, or a picture, or a piece of glass.[3]

This has the ring of genuineness about it. There is no difficulty in sympathising with such a point of view. The sentimental person is as nauseating in politics as in any other field of activity. Why, one might ask, should one want a Prime Minister to be sentimental?

We have quoted Edward Heath above (p. 54) as saying that, in his opinion, the emotions 'are things that warp judgement, and it is judgement which people want in a leader. That doesn't mean that I haven't got passionate personal interests and that there aren't other spheres in which you can have emotion.' The politician, like the doctor or the lawyer, in other words, should keep his work and his feelings separate.

But suppose, despite a politician's unceasing and skilful efforts to keep his private thoughts and feelings, his inner kingdom, always under lock and key, there should happen to be one small hole left through which we could continue to peer inside and see him without his public clothes on? Suppose this Peeping Tom's spy-glass were the Great Man's choice of metaphor, and that, by examining and classifying his metaphors we could identify the areas of life which were really important to him, the areas to which he turned instinctively for support when he needed to win an audience over to his way of thinking and feeling?

There is, however, a serious practical problem. Prime Ministers, unlike poets and Irish story-tellers, frequently employ other people to write their books, articles and speeches for them. Some, like Sir Anthony Eden, delivered speeches exactly as their ghosts had written them. Others – Baldwin, Bonar Law, Heath – preferred to work over other people's drafts, so that the final version of a speech contained a good deal of their own thoughts and personality. Others again – MacDonald, Attlee, Wilson, Lloyd George, Churchill – relied on civil servants and other functionaries to provide briefing material, but preferred to actually compose their speeches themselves, often moving from draft to draft and taking several days over the polishing and revision. In such instances, how much of the speech or the article came straight from the Prime Minister himself is often difficult to decide. There is certainly little point in either collecting or analysing the metaphors of his speechwriters, brilliant parrots as they sometimes are.

To play safe, it is wisest to confine one's quarryings to extempore utterances – press conferences, radio or television interviews, discussions – or to material produced before the great man became Prime Minister. Backbench Members are rarely rich enough to employ speechwriters, although one or two – Eden is the outstanding example – acquired the habit remarkably early in his Parliamentary career. Despite all possible caution, however, it is impossible to be absolutely sure that a 'characteristic' phrase or a sentence has not been suggested by someone else. Baldwin's celebrated sentence slaughtering the Beaverbrook and Rothermere press – 'what the proprietorship of these papers is aiming at is power, and power without responsibility, the prerogative of the harlot through the ages' – turns out to have been inspired by his cousin, Rudyard Kipling, although Baldwin was content to take the credit for it.

Speechwriting is a modern industry. Before the Second World War it was usually considered, in political and professional circles, to be distinctly low and American to hire a wordmonger to write one's speeches for one. Businessmen might do it, but then businessmen had no pretentions to personal culture. They were known to buy joke-books, in a pathetic attempt to raise a laugh at a dinner or the annual general meeting. If a politician of any calibre did occasionally stoop, under unusually great pressure of work, to paying an outsider to write a speech for him, he kept very quiet about it, and the speechwriter was expected to do the same. It was not the act of a gentleman and the man with a reputation to preserve knew this perfectly well.

For the Emperor of Metaphor, David Lloyd George, the employment of a speechwriter would have been not so much a disgrace as unthinkable. It would have removed one of the greatest pleasures and excitements in life, the proper exercise of one's talent for handling words. Although the present book is concerned mainly with the Sixties and Seventies, it is useful to throw one's glance a little further back in order to make certain modern developments easier to understand. On this particular point of political metaphor, the logical starting point is Lloyd George. Few men, inside or outside politics, have ever shown such a passion for metaphor as he did. His whole career, it might be said, was one vast metaphor. Yet, in his speaking, the images were, individually, of relatively small importance. It was the cumulative effect of what he was saying which caught the imagination of those who were listening to him, and for this reason a Lloyd George metaphor can often continue for a hundred words or more. Here is such a parable from his address to the Eisteddfod in August 1917:

> I have been in the habit once or twice of telling my fellow-countrymen, when there was anything that made them feel in the least depressed, to look upon the phenomenon of their hills. On a clear day they look as if they were near. You could reach them in a easy march – you could climb the highest of them in an hour. That is wrong – you could not. Then comes a cloudy day, and the mists fall upon them, and you say: 'There are no hills. They have

vanished.' Again you are wrong. The optimist is wrong; the hills are not as near as he thought. The pessimist is still more wrong, because they are there. All you have to do is to keep on. Keep on. Falter not. We have many dangerous marshes to cross; we will cross them. We have steep and stony paths to climb; we will climb them. Our footprints may be stained with blood, but we will reach the heights, and beyond them we shall see the rich valleys and plains of the new world which we have sacrificed so much to attain.

Nobody could read a dozen pages of Lloyd George's speeches without being aware of the part that the scenery and the climate of Wales played in his mental world. There is a never-ending cyclorama of mountains, clouds, storms, rivers, darkness and light, the indispensable background of the old Welsh preaching on which Lloyd George modelled his style. All this belongs to the on-stage part of his life. It tells us little about the man the public was not permitted to see, unless one chooses to believe – and it is not unreasonable – that these elemental-forces-of-nature images represent a form of sexual exhibitionism, a permitted opportunity to reveal the woman-longing, woman-conquering man that lay hidden inside the statesman's shell. Much more significant, perhaps, and either curiously or tactfully ignored by his biographers, are the metaphors of violence, the images drawn from the struggles of wild animals and from the battlefields where human beings destroy one another. His second wife, in her autobiography, has noted Lloyd George's obsession with battlefields. 'His great interest on visiting any country,' she recalls 'was to go to whatever battlefield presented itself, of whatever epoch, and reconstruct the fight.'[4]

His interest in fighting invariably finds an outlet in metaphors which focus on the brutality and bestiality of war, rather than on its technical refinements. The enemy is seen as a wolf or a tiger, and the task of the Allies was 'to tear the captured land free from the blood-stained claws'. German submarines were 'the wolves that prowled through the jungles of the deep', a merchant ship sailing to Britain was 'in the predicament of a swimmer in a shark-infested sea', Romania had to be 'rescued from the wolves that were tearing at her entrails', Belgium could well 'to plumb down the maw of another country', the Suez Canal was 'the jugular vein of the Empire', and France, 'rent deeply by the cruel claws of war', was 'bleeding from every vein, still on her feet facing the foe, but staggering'. In Russia, 'the Revolution was crouching just round the corner, and, as soon as the delegates left, it leapt up with a furious spring', and in Ireland it was necessary to 'cut the claws of the Sinn Fein movement'. Even the conservative, stolid British farmer was really no more than a wild animal lurking inside a human skin. When, under the conditions of war, he was ordered to plough up grassland, 'the grumbling became a growl and at last a smile with bared teeth'.

Given Lloyd George's background of Welsh folklore, it is possible that the pouncing, hostile, tearing creature that was so real and ever-present to him was a dragon, rather than a wolf. Whatever it was, the weapons were claws and teeth, not guns. Combat, in his imagination, was always a one-to-one affair, in which a young warrior, 'stripped bare for the fight', faced up bravely to a monster or prepared to 'thrust his spear under the fifth rib of Austria'. It took some time to bring these young warriors into fighting condition. On the outbreak of war, 'John Bull was getting soft, flabby and indolent. He was just slouching along. Then the war came and now his tissues are as firm as ever.'

There is no evidence that Lloyd George himself ever displayed any particular physical prowess or fondness for violence, either as a boy or a young man, or later in his life. As with Churchill, the fights-to-the-death of his dream-world have all the appearance of a compensation for the person he never was. The violence of his metaphors is by no means confined to fighting, however. To waver in one's determination to win the war was 'to put our heads into a noose with the rope end in the hands of Germany'. Serbia had 'dared to assassinate a future Emperor and deserved to be scourged. But it was too paltry a task for him to attend to the details of the lashing.' A thorough-going conscription policy had to reckon up 'the number of young men of military age who were fit to be thrown into the furnace to feed the flames of war'.

It may be true that, considering his political career as a whole, Lloyd George, in the words of his brother, 'spoke from the primitive emotions of the crowd, drawing his images from the elemental forces of nature and the incidents of common life, rarely travelling outside the experience of his audience'.[5] The secret of his popular appeal may have been his willingness to allow these primitive emotions to rise to the surface in the form of metaphors and parables. But not all his emotions and interests are primitive. Machines fascinated him – he enjoyed working with his hands, and envied the skilled workmen who were able to earn a living that way – and a considerable proportion of his images are drawn from the field of machinery. 'There are people', he said in 1917, 'who think the nation is like a petrol machine, that it can only be driven by a series of petty explosions, and unless they always hear it spluttering, they think the machine is at a standstill'.

Lloyd George, more than any other British Prime Minister except Churchill, is entitled to the enviable title of the man who hardly ever mixed a metaphor. One can search in vain through his speeches and books for the kind of nonsense that not infrequently fogs up the language of Wilson and Macmillan. Lloyd George does not, in the Wilson style, 'try to get the mercy corridor working', 'back the nuclear horse both ways', urge us to 'set our sights 1 per cent above last year', or to make sure that our efforts are 'properly dovetailed into the administrative machine'. Nor does he tie himself up in Macmillan's engaging nonsense. He could never have been responsible for such masterpieces of metaphorical muddle as 'The Budget was to be a milestone to Conservative victory and a tombstone in the Socialist graveyard. Now at last the tide of our fortunes was to turn and flow in our favour.'

Lloyd George would never have attracted or deserved the ridicule heaped on the present Prime Minister, James Callaghan, by the Leader of the Opposition: 'We have been promised that the next bright ploy will just hit the bullseye; that blue skies are just around the corner; that we will soon turn the corner; that the light is about to appear at the end of the tunnel – I quote from Mr. Callaghan's speeches of the past – that we are emerging from the valley of gloom; that we are heading for an economic miracle. We have had whole regiments of clichés marching into the sunset; but the problems just go on getting worse.'[6]

Lloyd George thought in metaphors. He did not tack them on afterwards, to brighten up the effect. It is interesting, for this reason, to note those of his habits and interests which never contributed to his stock of metaphors. We know, for instance, that throughout his life he admired and repeatedly re-read *Paradise Lost*, Burns, Macaulay, and Dickens. Yet his own speaking and writing contained no echoes from them. He was celebrated for his sensuality, but the human body provided exceedingly few of his metaphors. Domesticity meant a great deal to him, but, apart from one or two cat-images, there is almost nothing in his choice of metaphors to suggest it. Hearth and home, like Dickens and the female body, do not seem to have rivalled violence and battles in his fantasies. One can only suppose that the conscious part of his life could absorb them and deal with them satisfactorily. Sex was peripheral in his sub-conscious; violence was central.[7]

What then was the fantasy world of that other great trader in metaphor, Winston Churchill, a man 'universally admired, but little liked',[8] who had, unlike Lloyd George, a remarkable ability to impress his audiences but a much smaller talent for moving them. His life has been explored with some thoroughness,[9] although as yet not with the degree of objectivity and possibly irreverence which would allow adequate attention to be given to the less pleasing sides of his nature, admirably depicted in Graham Sutherland's great portrait, which the subject feared and hated for its truthfulness and which his widow burnt. The person emerging from these studies is a man yearning for praise and approval for his every action, suffering from long fits of depression, aggressive, unable to tolerate criticism of any kind and placing a high value on achieving comfort for himself at all times. Gluttonous, hard-drinking, and with a skin so soft and delicate that he could only wear silk next to it, working at hours which suited him and nobody else, a romantic demogogue who understood very little of the way ordinary people lived, this extraordinary creature is over-ripe for careful psychological investigation. What made him like this? What kind of boy turned into this kind of man?

The basic facts are known. Of small stature and undistinguished physique, he was neglected by his rich parents, sent to a major but not the leading public school, where he made little impression, either as a scholar or as a athlete, he joined the Army in South Africa and India, rather than a university in England, and developed a love of military affairs and an admiration for solidiers which remained with him all his life. Battles had a childish fascination for him. 'I love the bangs', he once said during a Second World War airraid, with complete honesty and apparently with total unawareness that many of his fellow citizens did not share his feelings, and on another occasion he referred to a couple of bullets as 'two soft kisses sucked in the air'. Language he loved – the English language. The mouthings of foreigners deserved only ridicule and contempt. He confessed to enjoying 'the feel of words fitting and falling into their places, like pennies in the slot', and he took great pains to avoid sloppy phrases and constructions himself and to criticise them in others.[10] The art of conversation was strange to him and he preferred monologues. Extempore speeches came under the headings of sloppiness. Every speech he made was worked over again and again until every word was to his satisfaction. He never gave interviews or press conferences.

What, if his metaphors are any guide, does the subconcious world of this boy in a man's body seem to have contained? A pattern is not easy to find, because the images are so abundant and because, in his anxiety to enliven his speeches at every point – he was essentially a rhetoretician – Churchill went for colour wherever he could find it. He has the usual politician's store-cupboard of purple words, well-stocked with storms, tides, dams, dawns, darkness and light, slippery slopes, Bible quotes and marching, but his great skill in putting sentences together often allows him to turn clichés into something a little more distinguished. 'Safety will be sturdy child of terror and survival the twin brother of annihilation' has very little meaning, but a great deal of polish.

Digging into his great mountain of metaphors, putting one-offs temporarily aside as curios and sorting the rest into batches and groups with similar characteristics, the Churchillian fantasy world gradually becomes more apparent. It is a violent world, inhabited by armed warriors, who are searching, sword in hand, for dragons and monsters in human shape to destroy. Sometimes, but not always, there is a fair maiden to rescue in the process. Single combat is the rule, blood flows generously, virtue always triumphs and the hero eventually receives the reward of his courage. The individuals and the countries he despises are often presented, in Communist fashion, as jackals and dogs ('This whipped jackal, Mussolini, comes frisking up at the sides of the German tiger'), but only Britain and her Empire are worthy of the lion symbol ('And now the old lion, with her lion cubs at her side, stands alone against hunters who are armed with deadly weapons and impelled by desperate and destructive rage').

This is surely how Churchill saw the world and his role in it. It was the compensation for his inadequacies as a child, and possibly also for the very low key of his sexual life. To say that he was a natural war-leader is to state the obvious. Peace uncovered his weaknesses and turned him into an inadequate schoolboy again, a sulky, disgruntled, unappealing schoolboy, throwing his carefully rehearsed bulldog expression against the world,[11] waiting for the next wave of armed champions to rush out onto the plain and break the intolerable monotony. For him, the significant times were those 'when nations are fighting for life, and everyone from prince to groom is fighting on the battlements'.

There are, even so, one or two significant minor groups among Churchill's metaphors – machines, food and drink, and swimming. Nature, in the form of plants, trees, flowers, domestic animals, appears hardly at all. There is no farming, no home life, and, strangely for a man whose main relaxations were bricklaying and painting, no building and almost no art. Painting, as Anthony Storr has pointed out,[12] became an important outlet for his aggression. It was as important to him as words, as a way of relieving the darkness of the depression into which he felt himself descending. In one remarkable passage.[13] Churchill refers to putting 'slashes of blue on the absolutely cowering canvas. Anyone could see that it could not hit back. No evil fate avenged the jaunty violence. The canvas grinned in helplessness before me. The spell was broken. The sickly inhibitions rolled away. I seized the largest brush and fell upon my victim with berserk fury. I have never felt in awe of a canvas since.'

There are virtually no Churchill sporting images of any kind and in this respect he is very different from Harold Macmillan, whose game-metaphors have been poured out in cheerful abundance during the whole of his adult life. There are boxing metaphors ('He was an agile antagonist and made rings round Bevan'); chess metaphors ('When one piece is moved in the delicate design of an administration, corresponding reactions follow, down to the humblest pawn'), and racing metaphors by the hundred ('Here was our greatest hero, the winning horse that we had bred and trained in our stable; and when the great day came it refused to run at all'; 'So we have got over this particular fence. The water-jump (the Suez Canal) is yet to come'). Cricket is much favoured. Concerning a series of negotations in New York, for example, he tells us, 'It was slow batting, not as good as a run a minute, but very safe play. Stumps were drawn at about 5 p.m.' Fishing is important to him ('Mr. Khruschev has taken the bait, but avoided the hook'), rabbiting and cock-fighting are not ignored ('In vain was the snare laid'; 'This Cock would not fight much longer'), hunting metaphors are frequent ('With the Afro-Asian pack in full cry, led on by the United States and Soviet Russia as joint masters'), and so are those drawn from boxing and fencing, ('Four armchairs for the protagonists, in middle of the room, with all the seconds, trainers, etc., ranged behind'; 'He had been so long accustomed to thrust that he had forgotten how to parry').

Mr. Macmillan does not seem to have enjoyed swimming a great deal. He comes across as a leisurely bather and paddler, rather than a vigorous swimmer. Toe-testing-the-water metaphors are numerous ('The Socialists, like cautious bathers, have just put a timorous toe into the water, and promptly withdrawn it'), but puzzles and conjuring obviously fascinated him. 'These,' he tells us, 'were the balls which the Chancellor of the Exchequer, like a Cinquevalli, was expected to keep in the air together', and one particular game, which he played in his youth, recurs again and again. In connection with Cyprus, for instance, 'The whole thing reminded me of one of those irritating puzzles that we had as children, when it was impossible to get all the balls into their respective holes at the same time. One could perhaps get in the Turks and the Greeks, but immediately Archbishop Makarios would suddenly pop out.'

Army life appears less in Macmillan's metaphors than one might have guessed, and when it does it is usually in a gentle form ('The final relief of the political sentries was preceded by nearly two years' manoeuvring'). Food and drink, on the other hand, are very important to him ('Cyprus goes on and off, like a dish in a cheap restaurant'; 'The world, starved of dollars and replete with sterling . . .'). One of his best continued metaphors, drawn from drink, is to be found in the maiden speech he made to the House of Commons in 1925. 'If he thinks,' said Macmillan of Ramsay MacDonald, 'that he and his party have only to offer us as the true socialism a kind of mixture, a sort of horrible political cocktail, consisting partly of the exploded economic views of Karl Marx, mixed up with a little flavour of Cobdenism, well-iced by the late Chancellor of the Exchequer, and with a little ginger from the Member from the Gorbals – if he thinks this is to be the draught given to our parched throats and that we are ready to accept it, he is very much mistaken.'

Sexual metaphors are found more frequently in the writings and speeches of Harold Macmillan than in those any other British Prime Minister of the last half century. A Minister is referred to as 'becoming impotent in the Department'; it was sad to observe 'the second rape of Czechoslovakia' and 'necessary to protect the virginity of Marxist Russia'. Marriage and babies are included in the mix. 'I observed,' he records, 'that although the proposed British marriage with Skybolt was not exactly a shotgun wedding, the virginity of the lady must now be regarded as doubtful', and he had watched with interest 'the feelings of intimate and almost loving care which every Chancellor bestows upon his yearly child'. And on another occasion he emphasises that 'the degree of inflation, like the housemaid's baby, was a very little one'.

As he grows older, metaphors connected with bodily disorders and doctors become much more frequent. He used them particularly to describe his attempts to deal with the troubles of the economy. 'One of the usual symptoms of a boom, that of unjustified wage demands, continued unchecked. For this expected persistence of high fever in spite of a low diet, a new term of art was later devised. . . . I seemed to get little support from the traditional forms of febrifuge – blood-letting, purging and the rest. I was therefore thrown back either on quack doctors or on an attempt, amid many other pre-occupations, to devise some new treatment by my own efforts.'

Throughout his life, this very Edwardian politician enjoyed the theatre and the circus and found relaxation in their colour and liveliness. It was natural for him to see his own retirement in an actor's terms. 'It has always seemed to me more artistic,' he wrote, 'when the curtain falls on the last performance, to accept the inevitable *E finita la commedia*. It is tempting, perhaps, but unrewarding, to hang about the greenroom after final retirement from the stage.'

Mr. Macmillan's speeches have not, alas, always remained entirely immune to that major political nuisance, the mixed metaphor disease. He has in his time perpetrated such unworthy expressions of non-thinking as:

'If he plays his cards well (Bonomi) can turn the tables on the Italian Communists. They are on the horns of a dilemma.'
'The Budget was to be a milestone to Conservative victory and a tombstone in the Socialist graveyard. Now at last the tide of our fortunes was to turn in our favour.'
'We were flexing our muscles in an increasingly rigid mould.'
'A long innings by a Government which has been thrown about like a rudderless ship in a storm.'

In fairness to Mr. Macmillan, one should point out that it is only rarely that he loses control to such an extent. Sir Harold Wilson is a much more frequent offender in this respect. The former Labour leader has the reputation of being a clever phrase-man, using brilliant epigrams and dazzlingly contrived figures of speech to annoy and demolish his opponents. Some of his bon-mots have unfortunately gone down, if not into history, at least into the anthologies and card-indexes from which history is written. He has a sharp edge, but on more than one occasion his over-bright metaphors have got him into serious trouble. Loyalty to the leader and the Party is one thing, but there were, as it turned out, certain dangers in comparing the dissenters and nuisances to dogs. 'Every dog', he declared, waiting carefully for the applause, 'is allowed one bite, but if biting becomes too much of a habit, its owner tends to have doubts about renewing the licence when it comes up.' The thought was not popular among sections of the Party and explanations were subsequently demanded. The really effective metaphor, even in politics, should not require a softening translation or apology.

The well-cultivated public image of gentle, kindly Harold Wilson, the poor butcher, unable to bring himself to sack even the most grossly inefficient of ministers, may need a little revision, if one large group of his metaphors is any guide. 'He comes,' says Wilson in a characteristically friendly way of a Conservative opponent, 'and carves another hunk of flesh from the Welfare State and throws it to the wolves to buy time for a few months.' In his speeches there is a good deal of cutting, chopping and tearing apart. Even cuddly, clubbable George Brown is recorded as having 'sweated blood with Donnelly'.

Sporting metaphors are abundantly on hand, however, to provide some sort of antidote to the violence. We have 'the Chancellor, who played the bowling with a very straight bat', and history, which 'was full of top-rank centre-forwards relegated to the reserves for failing to stop a shot at goal for fear of missing'. Wilson, true to his image of the Yorkshire Man of the People, has always loved cricketing metaphors and often develops them at great length. 'The Government have been enjoying for the past three years a batsman's wicket and now the batsman's wicket is crumbling a bit. The Chancellor's own reputation as a batsman is due far more to the wicket than to his ability in using the bat. Indeed, now that the Chancellor is discarding it during this period, by dismantling controls and deciding to throw away his bat altogether and rely on his pads, I would remind him of the fate of the five English batsmen, in the fate of the first innings of the Test Match which ended today.'

Wilson can handle cricket and football, the people's games, but he is liable to get a bit confused when he ventures into the pastimes of the élite. 'I loved the debates,' he tells us. 'It was real rapier stuff, and sometimes I landed up flat on my back, sometimes him.' Swordsmen and fencers, unlike boxers and wrestlers, are not in the habit of knocking their opponents flat on their backs. Dancing, too, shows him uncertain of his facts. 'Too much effort,' he believed, 'was going into the delicate footwork, through Brussels and WEU, which constituted what I called the European quadrille, when the dance-hall proprietor had already made it clear that there was going to be no dance.' Quadrilles, one has to remind Mr. Wilson, were performed in elegant ballrooms, not in dance-halls. His passion for democracy sometimes played tricks with his imagery, and now and again one is bound to wonder if he really thinks about the meaning of words at all. Nixon, to him, was 'a man who had been through the political treadmill' – convicts were put on a treadmill, not through it, which would have been painful – and if he had indeed 'had experience of what the grass-roots could do to Mr. Smith', Mr. Smith surely deserves our sympathy, because all that roots can do to people is to grow in them.

Harold Wilson's arch-opponent for a number of years, Edward Heath, has never bubbled over with metaphors. There is, in fact, only one important category of Health metaphor, and it takes a long time to collect a dozen examples even of this. It is concerned, not unexpectedly, with boats and sailing, and it is possible this is the equivalent of Wilson's cricket and football, the Prime Minister as his P.R. man would like the nation to see him. This Edward Heath believes in 'a form of government in which you don't veer violently', and sympathises with 'employers who found it necessary to stand men off in order to keep themselves afloat'.

Margaret Laing has noted[14] that talking was not encouraged in the Heath home and that one result of this was 'to exaggerate an inherited tendency towards brevity of speech, and to render him inhibited, and even inarticulate when it came to discussing, or even expressing, deep personal feelings and problems.' She agrees with the often-made comparison between Heath and a computer – feed him with information and wait for the print-out of the answer. The silences occur when the computer is badly programmed and, in Heath's terms, to ask what he feels about something or someone is to programme him incompetently.

Lord Avon (Sir Anthony Eden) had a number of characteristics in common with Mr. Heath. Overwhelmed by his 'intensely masculine',[15] eccentric, boxing-enthusiast father, he always took great pains to keep his private life private. 'No epigram or witticism has ever been attributed to him,' says his biographer, 'nor has he ever employed any memorable phrase.'[16] Certainly nothing to equal Macmillan's 'It rained umbrellas', or Lloyd George's 'France, with her face all wrinkled with Party lines', or Baldwin's 'I met Curzon in Downing Street, from whom I got a very chilly nod and the sort of feeling a corpse would give an undertaker'. Eden always covered his tracks with great care. His later speeches were often, perhaps usually, ghost-written, but he is believed to have composed his maiden House of Commons speech himself. The theme was air-defence. It was dull and safe, and his speech-writers had no difficulty in recapturing the authentic tone and flavour. Yet in one place the man shows through. 'It is a natural temptation to honourable members opposite', he began, 'some of whose views on defence were fairly well known during the years of the war, to adopt the attitude of that very useful domestic animal, the terrier, and roll on their backs and wave their paws in the air with a pathetic expression.' It was a metaphor that might well have come from his sport-loving father, and a high proportion of his own metaphors are indeed drawn from riding and hunting. A question put to a prospective Member by a constituency selection committee was 'the last fence which the candidate had to get over'. A person responsible for a bad political blunder 'is like a bad rider who drives his spurs into a horse and the next minute jabs it in the mouth and, when the poor brute gets into a muck sweat sweat, beats it and says, "what a rotten horse you are", while it is really the rider who is both arrogant and inept.' The metaphor is not one which would come either easily or accurately to a Left-wing representative of the urban working-class.

Eden's other main metaphor-groups are sensual and related mainly to smoothing, rubbing, stroking and eating. Molotov 'did what he could to rub off some of the sharp angles', but at the end of the conference they had to admit that there were 'matters that cannot be ironed out between us'. Another conference met 'to discuss what is very thin gruel indeed', during the war there were 'committees that fed the Defence Committee', and in 1956 he remarked that 'the Russians have brought us an actual shopping list'.

Not memorable phrases, perhaps, but something a little more lively than the officialese which made up the average Eden offering to his colleagues and the public. Both in speaking and writing, he was much given to the double-negative, that time-honoured screen between a politician and civil servant and the world. Randolph Churchill believed this showed 'a psychological fear of the positive',[17] and this may well be so. To use clear, direct language and strong, sharp images is to commit oneself, a dangerous step for any politician to take. A good poet cannot be a good politician, at least nowadays. And to commit oneself is a mark of confidence, of a belief in what one is doing. The public figure whose language is woolly is a person whose language has to be woolly, if he is to talk at all, because he has nothing positive to say.

Ramsay MacDonald is an excellent illustration of this sad truth. 'His style,' it has been said, 'deteriorated as he became entangled in political compromises'.[18] The early MacDonald, steeped in the Bible and Socialist theory, passionately interested in biology and geology and wholly dedicated to the working-class cause, had a well-organised mind and a straightforward way of expressing himself. The MacDonald of the Twenties and Thirties, a considerable social figure and a politician determined to hold on to power at all costs, had nothing to say and a great deal to conceal. He did both at great length. While he still held firmly to his Socialist faith, or, as his enemies preferred to put it, before he allowed himself to be corrupted, his language remained pretty well under control, although even as a young man there were signs of the chaos into which his words were later to fall. In view of subsequent developments, one cannot be entirely happy about such sentences as, 'Upon their gross materialist roots grow fine spiritual blossoms, on the solid rough foundation rise pinnacles of divine ideas stretching upward to heaven'.

At every period of his life, however, MacDonald enjoyed playing with words quite as much as Lloyd George did. He drew heavily on the Bible for his imagery, his vocabulary and his rhythms ('The working-class Radicalism of the sixties was the salt of the earth'; 'Time runs, but how empty his hands are of gathered sheaves'; 'Poverty is always at his door, uncertainty sits with him in his home'), but equally important for him during the years before 1914 was his conviction that society was a biological organism, to which only Socialism could give adequate political expression. A favourite thought, repeated hundreds of times in his books and speeches, was that 'the individual is primarily a cell in the organism of his Society'. Within Society, 'though the diseased functions atrophy, they retain a sort of parasitic life and maintain a ceremonial and social existence owing to the incapacity of the social organism to throw them off completely'.

Yet he saw society in many other shapes. At one time it was 'a cannibal-battle royal', and at others a river ('the swift and straight running current of Socialism'), a 'hive of busy workers', or a 'machine which is always getting out of gear'. As the years went on and the war destroyed his beliefs, none of these pictures – and like Lloyd George, he lived by pictures – satisfied him, and he began to superimpose one widely on top of another, as if hoping that some kind of Identikit meaning would result. 'If the people cannot construct Socialism in their minds,' he wrote, 'then they cannot build it into their institutions'. And in his own attempt to build Socialism in his mind, he rushed in desperation from one metaphor to another, hoping each time that if harvests and weeds failed to yield the golden answer, then bugle calls and battering rams, or gardeners and pruning hooks might do so. The true tragedy of MacDonald was not that he deserted the parlours of the workers for the drawing rooms of the rich, but that he never found that completely satisfying metaphors to explain the essence of humanity to him.

The five Prime Ministers who form what might be termed the quiet group of post-First World War politics in Britain – Bonar Law, Baldwin, Neville Chamberlain, Attlee, Douglas-Home – seem to have lived relatively happily without a metaphorical core to their lives, much as some men appear to manage very well without sex or alcohol. This is not to say that they were incapable of producing or enjoying a neat turn of phrase, or that we cannot learn a good deal about them by discovering the fields from which they draw their metaphors and those which they avoid. Baldwin, for instance, with his horror of social life, his uneasiness in the company of women, his fondness for agriculture and the English countryside, very naturally concentrates on images taken from domestic life and the farmyard. He was not, he said, 'on the whole disposed to conclude that the people are such a helpless, ineffective flock of sheep', but he had watched, with abhorrence, the war-time politicians 'leading reluctant and unsuspecting people into the shambles'. He disliked and mistrusted the Labour Party, not because of its philosophy, but because it was not, in his opinion, 'a comfortable household'. In the Labour Party, 'there are so many occasions when the peace of the home is rudely shattered by some of the boisterous and ecstatic children bursting into shrieks or falling into paroxysms, which are offensive to the ears of their parents and their more sedate brothers, as they are to their neighbours in the surrounding tenements'.

There are no violent metaphors in Baldwin, no wolves tearing people to pieces, no stabbings, either in the back or in the front, no swords or massacres. And there are none in Sir Alec Douglas-Home, either. This Prime Minister from the grouse moors confines himself to the quite browns and greens of life. 'I think,' he says, 'that we ought to have a good shot at it', and he has certain demands to make, 'if this (the Government) is to be a genuine club.' Commonwealth trade preferences 'have been eroded away a bit'. President John F. Kennedy 'bore on his shoulders all the cares and the hopes of the world', and his death was one of the 'times in life when mind and heart stand still'.

Bonar Law, Presbyterian, lifelong teetotaller, star of a Glasgow debating society, partner in a merchant bank, relied, for the most part, on metaphors from fishing ('The hon. member laid his baits for the applause of the gentlemen around him') and from building ('They pull down the house in order to improve the ventilation'). Lord Attlee, too, the man who punctured Churchill's oratory time and time again with terse, abrupt questions, rarely rose very much above his low-key, domestic cruising level. He was accustomed to 'sitting by the bedside of dying or dead industries', observed 'the Lord Privy Seal, who, with difficulty, kept his feeble infant alive from week to week', and believed that, 'seeing the amount of cloth available, we had to see what kind of a coat we could produce'. There are very occasional Biblical echoes ('the provision for Lazarus of some crumbs from the rich man's table'), a below-average proportion of clichés ('to see everything through Russian spectacles'; 'he kept close to the beating heart of the people') and many metaphors of a homely, domestic type, with a strong emphasis on gardening. Like Lord Avon and Mr. Harold Macmillan, who also served throughout the First World War, Lord Attlee makes little use of his military experiences as a source of metaphors. Unlike Lloyd George and Churchill, who were romantics and revelled in war, these three seemed glad to put the heroics and suffering of wartime behind them and to become the ex-officer type of civilian which existed in plenty during the Twenties and Thirties.

To approach a man through his metaphors is a technique pioneered many years ago by the Shakespearian scholar, Caroline Spurgeon. Shakespeare left very slender clues to his upbringing, career and private life, and Dr. Spurgeon's technique, developed long before the days of the computer and the grotesque excesses of sexual psychology, consisted of a careful classification of all the metaphors of the plays and the poems, so that one might be in a position to make intelligent guesses at certain features of the poet's life which would otherwise have remained hidden. There are certain important differences between Sir Harold Wilson or Earl Baldwin and Shakespeare, but there may be some value in applying similar methods of investigation to a body of people whose private lives and thought have been a matter of much greater public curiosity than Shakespeare ever needed to defend himself against. What kind of a wall an Elizabethan would have constructed around himself in order to protect himself against the probings of journalists and interviewers, had such inquisitiveness existed 350 years ago, is difficult to say. But it is possible to suggest that Dr. Spurgeon, digging into Shakespeare, had a considerably easier task than a modern investigator digging into Heath or Wilson, mainly because the great majority of Shakespeare's metaphors are alive, whereas a twentieth century politician – Churchill was the great exception – will almost certainly offer at least a dozen utterly worn-out metaphors for every one that still has flavour and vitality. There is little point in collecting and analysing clichés and muddles, so a preliminary sifting of the wheat from the chaff is essential.

Image-analysis can be interesting to students of both politics and human nature, and not only, of course, with British raw material to work on. A similar study of the metaphors of, say, Adolf Hitler or Richard Nixon, made early enough in their careers, might have saved their respective countries, and the world, a great deal of unnecessary suffering. A CIA or MI5 concerned with the minute study of the metaphors of public men could quite well do considerably more good than the heresy and conspiracy hunts which are often confused with security measures today. International Metaphor Intelligence would be a most valuable political innovation, in the best interests of humanity.

8 Government Public Relations

When people use the term 'Government Public Relations', they may be referring to four quite separate things. First, they may mean, if the country is Britain, the publicity service of Transport House, if the Labour Party is in power, or of the Conservative Central Office, if control of the nation's affairs at the moment lies with the Conservative Party. The Parties run their own propaganda organisations which are financed from Party and not public funds. Secondly, there are what a Director of the Central Office of Information, Sir Robert Fraser, once described as 'the Government's own relations with the public, the quality of the personal lines with the people which the Ministers of any Government must have, and the goodness or badness of which will be determined by the flair, personalities and the programme of the men who form the Administration'.[1] As Sir Robert goes on to point out: 'Government Public Relations in this sense existed long before anyone had thought of Directors of Public Relations or Official Information Services. If you had said to Disraeli or Gladstone or Joseph Chamberlain, "You are faced with an acute problem of public relations", they would not have understood what you were talking about. They conducted their own relations with the public and expected to do so as part of their political leadership.'

Thirdly, there is the purely Departmental aspect of public relations. Like ICI or IBM or the United States Steel Corporation, a large Government Department is necessarily interested in maintaining good relations with the people with whom it deals, between the organisation and the public. The fourth type of Government public relations consists of the officially and publicly financed Information Services. In Britain, these were set up during the Second World War for propaganda and publicity purposes and not disbanded afterwards, although nowadays they run on a comparatively small budget and small staff. The Central Office of

Information is not a policy-making body. It exists only as a service department, producing information and publicity material for other Government Departments which require them. When it was first established the C.O.I., or rather its wartime predecessor, was taken as evidence that 'for the first time the Government was consciously accepting some measure of responsibility for seeing that a fully enfranchised people confronted with manifold and difficult problems, received all the information they needed in order to make up their minds about the answers and generally to act as intelligent citizens.'[2] The aim was laudable, the achievement slightly less so, no doubt as a result of shortcomings on the part of the public.

Of these four different kinds of Government public relations, the first three are certain to present biased information – they are in business to sell the Government and its agencies in one way or another – and the fourth, although in itself impartial, must necessarily function for a large part of the time as a manufacturer and distributor of reflections of the official point of view. Consequently, the amount of reliable, neutral information which the public receives is relatively small. Both at home and abroad, the Government, as a whole and through its major Departments, is naturally anxious to create as favourable an impression as possible. This has always been the case. It is not a recent development.

In Britain, the real beginning of anything that can be called organised public relations is usually considered to have been the establishment of the Empire Marketing Board in 1926. The Board had an able Director, Sir Stephen Tallents, an annual budget, and a clearly defined aim, 'to bring the Empire alive to the minds of people in Britain'. Its work was essentially promotional. There is no evidence that Tallents ever tried very hard or very systematically to discover what British people thought and felt about the Empire. His job, as he saw it – and few people would have disagreed with him – was to use every technique at his disposal to tell his fellow-countrymen what went on in the Empire, or at least the more reputable things that went on, and to stimulate an interest in countries to which most of the public had never been and were never likely to go, but whose products they might be encouraged to buy. It was essentially a selling exercise; it marketed the Empire.

Tallents continued his policy of using the best available artists, film makers, photographers, writers and other experts, when he became Public Relations Officer to the Post Office in 1933. This appointment is generally reckoned to mark the first use of the term 'Public Relations Officer' in Britain and to have been introduced from America by Sir Kingsley Wood, who was Postmaster-General at the time.

By contrast with those who run Government public relations today, Tallents had an easy job. Neither with the Empire Marketing Board nor with the Post Office did he have to win over a hostile public. In the Twenties and Thirties people were, on the whole, well disposed both to the Empire and the Post Office. Children still celebrated Empire Day at school, there was as yet little feeling of guilt about having an Empire, the Mother-Country was showing no signs of wanting to rid herself of her overseas possessions, George V continued to be the King-Emperor, Rudyard Kipling was a respected figure, the P. and O. and Union Castle lines maintained the Imperial transport links, the Indian Army was intact, and the black, brown and yellow people ruled over by the British Crown were as exotic and romantic as they had always been. Tallents had splendid material to work with and he made the most of it.

The Post Office used to be similarly placed. Before the Second World War the British were rightly proud of their Post Office. It provided a cheap, reliable service, and the postman, like the policeman, was the people's friend and it was customary to give him a Christmas present as a token of one's esteem and gratitude. By present-day standards, there were an incredible number of collections and deliveries each day, and for a letter or parcel to fail to arrive or to be misdelivered was almost the end of the world, a situation demanding questions in Parliament and the carpeting or dismissal of officials. Had Sir Stephen Tallents been in charge of public relations at the Post Office today, he would have found himself faced with the need to put a good face on a steadily deteriorating service and to placate highly critical customers. He would be required to promote what every public relations man dreads, a bad product.

One has to distinguish, so far as this is possible, between public relations and information. This is information:

Contributions to the new pensions scheme start in April 1978. From April 1979 pensions will be in two parts. A basic pension, like the present retirement pension, will be paid by the State. An additional pension, related to each employee's earnings, will be paid either by the State or by an employer's pension scheme.

> Because of this changes are being made to contributions – see leaflet NP 34.
>
> If you carry on working after the normal retirement age (65 for men, 60 for women) you will no longer have to pay contributions. But you will need a 'certificate of age exception' to give to your employer so that he does not mistakenly deduct contributions. You should get one of these certificates automatically if you reach pension age *after* 6 April 1978 and carry on working. But if you do not receive one, or you reach pension age *before* 6 April 1978, you can get one by asking your local social security office. If your employer wrongly deducts contributions you will have to ask him for a refund. If you have more than one employer you will need a certificate for each of them.[3]

and this is public relations:

> Old age pensions will go up again in November, for the fourth time since Labour took office; thousands of old people are helped by Supplementary Benefits; the earnings rule for widows has been abolished.
>
> The Superannuation Bill, which we will re-introduce, will abolish poverty among the aged within twenty years. It will provide a pension guaranteed against inflation, and will end the financial discrimination against women.
>
> Labour has increased family allowances 3 times in 6 years; the Tories did not do it during their last 8 years. Recent large increases will direct aid where it is most needed, and help solve the problem of child poverty.
>
> Redundancy payments, combined with the supplement to unemployment benefit, will give many more people the chance to take time over choosing a new job.[4]

The first kind of Government handout eventually, sometimes very soon, provides raw material for the second: the message being 'Look what we have done for you'. By no means all official information material is capable of being used in this way, of course. Most of the brochures, leaflets and reports issued by governments and government departments are strictly practical. They will range from details of new postal charges, to budgetary statements, and from exchange regulations to recommendations for new agricultural techniques. Any of this material is potentially controversial, simply because there are bound to be some people, perhaps many, who will disagree with certain aspects of it or be annoyed by it. But its prime purpose is to give information to those who are judged to need it. The level on which the information is presented will depend on the assessment of the market. Sometimes this is badly judged and the result is confusion and frustration. The audience simply cannot understand what it is being told.

As Tom Harrisson put it, after many years research into the attitudes and behaviour of ordinary people, our society still contains a frightening number of Don't Knows. 'They genuinely don't know', he said, 'largely because so much of the stuff put out in our democracy goes over their heads or passes them by. It is not necessarily that they don't want to know. But when they try to find out (for instance from a Government White Paper) the language defeats them right at the start. . . . It is extraordinary what large sections even of the mass newspapers are not read or absorbed except by an active minority – or by, as we might call it, the informed tenth.'[5]

Harrisson wrote this thirty years ago and it would be a brave optimist who believed that the situation had changed a great deal since. The problem remains, and Harrisson defined it very neatly when he declared that 'modern democracy is certainly not in a position to have many of its citizens as slot-mechanical spectators semi-supine on the side-line'. But that, alas, is precisely what it has got and no way, as yet, has been found of getting round the problem, always assuming that those in charge of the nation's affairs, any nation's affairs, would welcome a well-informed, politically wide-awake electorate. Governments have a split mind on this point. On the one hand they say and, at the time they say it, probably mean that people should be adequately briefed about the multitude of topics, at home and abroad, that affect their lives and well-being. On the other, they are conscious of the fact that governments are brought to power and kept in power by what the public feels quite as much as by what it knows and that the manipulation of the emotions is a politician's prime talent. It is, of course, perfectly possible to have a well-filled head as well as a warm heart, but the tradition in politics has always been to try to provide just sufficient facts to persuade voters that they are making a rational choice and to condition the public to interpret these facts in a way that will cause the right candidate to be elected.

If politics were a purely intellectual affair and if the electorate spent a regular number of hours each week quietly accumulating the evidence they needed to arrive at a wise decision, election campaigns would indeed be a complete waste of time. In the privacy of their own homes, people would place fact against fact, consult the opinions of their family and friends, and go serenely to the ballot box to register their support for the candidate judged most worthy of their confidence. This is not, alas, how things happen. In Britain – the situation is not quite the same in America – the pattern of political opinion changes very little from decade to decade. In broad terms, voting follows family tradition, financial status and occupation. Few Conservative voters are to be found among unskilled manual workers and few Labour voters among bank managers, accountants and West End hairdressers. The voting-swings which are so much prayed for by all parties are caused mainly by three factors – the Don't Knows miraculously making up their minds to vote, the politically idle deciding to leave their fireside chairs and walk to the nearest school or church hall to put a cross on a piece of paper, fold it up and drop it into a steel box – an enormous effort, which exhausts their five-year ration of political energy – and the waverers, who have been annoyed or disgusted by something, quite often trivial or irrelevant, which a public figure has done or said during the run-up to the election. The election campaign itself is a side-show, which breaks the monotony of existence for a brief period, encourages a mild orgy of prejudice-letting, and then disappears to leave the surface of the nation as unrippled as it found it. For those who take politics seriously it is a disappointing business.

The situation as it really is bears little relation to what is described in scholarly works on politics, of which the following paragraph can be taken as a reasonably typical example.

> The liberal model of English politics demands a great flow of information between governors and governed. The greater the supply of information, the better informed the public and, as the public is supposed to be the ultimate arbiter of policy, the better the policies of government. In the liberal model government is expected to supply information freely to governed because the public has 'a right to know'. The Whitehall model of communication, by contrast, has a very different view of supply-demand relationships. Information is assumed to be a scarce commodity and, like all scarce commodities, it is not freely exchanged.[6]

As we have said above, information and public relations are not the same thing. Public relations is the deliberate art of creating a good impression. The information provided by official bodies may or may not contribute towards that good impression. Public relations is not necessarily a matter of words at all. If politicians want to win friends, as they certainly do, their manner and appearance are quite as important as the content of any statement they may make. The most effective and deep-penetrating public relations probably has little to do with words at all. If a member of the public says of, say, a Cabinet Minister, 'I wouldn't trust that man an inch', 'She doesn't sound sincere', 'Too smooth by half', or 'You can see he's knocking it back nowadays', that Minister can say farewell to at least one political supporter, no matter how well he presents the Government's case. If he sounds 'too intellectual', 'too public school', or 'too uneducated', he will have made another enemy there, too. One cannot, of course, please everybody, but if 50.1 per cent of those who vote find the candidate not impossibly unpleasant or sinister and 49.9 per cent dislike him on sight there is no great need to worry.

What is certainly absurd is to pretend that Government public relations is purely and simply a matter of what Professor Rose calls 'a great flow of information between governors and governed', unless one chooses to interpret 'information' in a much wider sense than Professor Rose intended. 'We do not,' as one American linguist has pointed out recently, 'talk only with our mouths. The non-verbal component of human communication is as vital to the message as the verbal component.'[7] If a politician, however exalted, comes across to television viewers as shifty, mean, greedy, bored, unscrupulous or an automaton, no amount of brilliant phraseology or deep thinking is going to put matters right. The television impression is part of the 'great flow of information' and the public relations experts are, much to their regret, stuck with it. Suppose, however, that we confine ourselves to information in its narrow sense of facts. For whom are these facts intended and what kind of people are anxious to have them? In the first place, for journalists, with their self-appointed role of watchdogs in the public interest. The journalist sees himself as a ferret, whose daily task is to be put into burrows by his editor in order to flush out the rabbits inside. The unwilling rabbits, not unnaturally, will do everything in their power to dodge the ferret and the game of journalism, or part of it, is played in these terms. Once the ferret-journalist has unearthed his information, he earns the remainder of his living by processing it for public consumption. This is the process known as 'keeping the public informed'. But the facts themselves are not sufficient. They have to be sifted, shaped and flavoured to make them 'interesting', so that the journalist's public will want to read them. Whether the version of the 'information' which is finally presented to readers, viewers and listeners bears any relation to what was discovered in the first place is a matter of pure chance. Information, in this sense, can be compared to a consignment of flour, some of which will fall into the hands of cooks who will incorporate it into a decent, honest cake or pie-crust, and some who will produce from it a disgusting confection which can hardly be brought under the heading of food at all.

It is certainly true to say that a democratic society does depend on a steady flow of information between governors and governed, but it is one thing to provide the information and quite another to persuade people to accept it, like it and be interested in it. Some people will behave as theory says they should behave, they will work away at what they are given until they understand it, they will ask questions and discuss and eventually add to their stock of knowledge what they have digested. There are those who have a professional reason for doing this. Economists, for instance, are obliged to study the official reports which contain material relevant to their speciality. Legal changes embodies in new Acts of Parliament are vital to the industries and occupations they directly affect. Retail business and manufacturers must be accurately informed about the provisions of the Trades Descriptions Act. Exporters must be careful not to fall foul of the law when they are shipping their goods abroad and arranging for payment. All this is an essential part of running any kind of modern state and the information concerning it has little to do with the matter of Government public relations, except in so far as the regulations are found to be sensible or irritating.

Not infrequently, very desirable changes in the law are not made because, in the opinion of the Party managers and advisers, they would create political problems and lose votes. Excellent examples of this can be found in the field of motor transport. In Britain, where large numbers of people choose to run or are forced to run motorcars without really being able to afford to do so, the minimum standard of vehicle maintenance and driving performance required by law is absurdly and dangerously low. If, however, the level were to be raised to, say, that insisted on for London taxicabs and taxidrivers, half the drivers and cars in the country would be off the road, and rightly so. That would cause an outcry of such ferocity that the Government responsible would undoubtedly find political survival difficult. So, in the politicians' interests of holding on to power, dangerous vehicles and dangerous drivers are tolerated. Exactly the same is true of restaurants and cafés which fail to meet the legal standards of hygiene. The Government inspectors know perfectly well that if they did what they are supposed to do, that is, if eating places were forced to obey the regulations, three-quarters at least would find the task impossible and would have to close down. This in turn would mean that, at least in the short term, the nation would have nowhere to eat, except at home, where the conditions are often worse than in any public restaurant, but where the law does not operate. So the regulations are not stringently enforced, in the hope that time will show a gradual improvement. Politics, as we have been reminded for so long, is the art of the possible, and any government or party which insisted on the impossible would not last long.

This amounts to saying that satisfactory Government public relations often demands that the law shall be disregarded. The police have a legal duty to measure the depth of tyre treads which they suspect to be below the legal minimum; they very rarely do so. On the occasion of industrial disputes, all picketing, to remain within the law, has to be 'peaceful' and to be limited to 'persuasion'; it is often extremely violent and threatening, but no action is taken, because the Government is unwilling to antagonise or, as the current political jargon has it, 'provoke' the Trades Unions in any way. On these matters, therefore, what is judged to be politically prudent takes precedence over what the law says should happen, and that is a very interesting kind of public relations.

It cannot always be easy for a government to forecast with any certainty which of its activities, disclosures or publications will take the fancy of journalists, and therefore receive prominence in the media, and which will be filed away without any publicity being given to them. The unexpected may sometimes turn out to be welcome, sometimes not. Consider, for example, a Ministry of Agriculture booklet, *Exemptions from Ingredient Listing and Generic Terms*, which appeared early in 1978. The title is not immediately appealing and even the most enterprising and sharp-eyed reporter could be excused for overlooking it. Yet, *The Times*[8] gave it a noble ration of space, under the heading, 'Telling us what we eat, in Plain

English'. The report came, it appears, from the Food Standards Committee, which advises the Government on the need to change the legislation relating to food and drink. As *The Times* says, 'the chaste appearance and forbidding title belie the revolutionary contents of the report', which says bluntly that 'as a matter of principle, there should no longer be any exemption from ingredient declaration' and the descriptions of many ingredients should be made more precise and helpful to the customer. The Committee rejects industrial objections to its proposals and foresees lists of ingredients on boxes of chocolates, packets of cheese, half-pounds of butter and bottles of whisky. 'Not only is the document interesting and understandable,' comments *The Times*, 'it is also distributed free'.

This amounts to excellent public relations, both for the Government and the Ministry of Agriculture, which emerge from the report and from the newspaper publicity given to it as friends of the consumer, anxious to do everything possible to make sure that people know exactly what they are eating and prepared to defy vested interests in order to bring this about. But this is bonus public relations, public relations without deliberate intent. No member of the government and no civil servant, so far as one knows, has promoted the report as a likely vote-winner or taken pains to make sure that it is written in a way which will make the greatest possible number of friends and the fewest enemies. No-one is likely to monitor the reception of the report in order to find out what the public thinks of it.

Almost anything which is done in the name of the Government can affect its standing in the country, anything can have political implications, even if these were never intended. I well remember being invited to address officers and ratings at a Naval training establishment and being told by the Captain that I must say nothing political. 'Is it permitted,' I asked him, 'to observe that the seat of your trousers is shiny?' 'What,' he enquired, 'has that to do with it?' 'Everything', I pointed out to him, 'because to make such a comment would be to be guilty of a highly political statement. It could be taken to imply that naval officers are so grossly underpaid by a hostile Government that they cannot afford to buy themselves new trousers. By pointing out that your trousers are shiny, I could be making a strong criticism of the Government and the policies for which it stands.'

The point is not a trivial one. Any government can spend large sums of money in attempts to create a favourable public image of itself, only to find that many of the factors which determine that image are accidental and quite outside its control. One could put this another way by saying that although Public Relations, in the narrow and formal sense, may have a language, style and set of rules which are laid down by authority, public relations is happening all the time on its own. The most unlikely the unplanned statement can influence opinion for or against the government in power.

Consider, for instance, the most innocent-looking Government publication I have been able to find, *National Savings for You*.[9] This is a 14-page booklet, drawn up to explain precisely and simply what forms of saving are available and how one makes use of them. Nothing, one might think, could be more objective and politically neutral, and most of the information provided is, indeed, of this order. But not all. Suppose, for example, one looks carefully at the subsection, headed 'Withdrawals'. It reads:

> You may make one withdrawal a day, in cash, of up to £30 on demand at any savings bank post office, but the bank book will be impounded if the withdrawal exceeds £20. If you make two withdrawals on demand each of over £10 within seven days, the paying officer will retain the bank book for examination at Savings Bank Headquarters. This rule applies even if the book has been examined between the dates of the two withdrawals. To withdraw, in cash, a sum of over £30, you must apply on a notice of withdrawal. If you require a crossed warrant, similar to a cheque, you must apply on a notice of withdrawal and you must send the bank book with the form. The minimum sum for which a crossed warrant will be issued is £1.

The information itself is clear enough, but it would not be unreasonable for anyone reading this section to feel that he was in contact with a ridiculously bureaucratic system, the main aim of which was to create as many jobs as possible and to cause the maximum of inconvenience to people with a National Savings Bank Account. 'Why,' he might well ask, 'is it so simple to draw money out of an ordinary banking account, and so extraordinarily difficult in the case of the system run by the Government? Why is it impossible for the Post Office to provide cheque books? Why this extraordinary, time-consuming Victorian procedure of continually sending in one's bank book to headquarters?' While trying to find the answers to these questions, he might well conclude that fatuous bureaucracy and old-fashioned methods were inseparable from anything run by Government agencies. He might also decide that, since nothing had been done to modernise the Savings Bank's methods during the years in which the Labour Government had been in power, the Government and the Labour Party might well prefer things the way they were. In that case, this little booklet was one further package of evidence of the essentially bureaucratic, unenterprising nature of the Labour Government, and that, because the workings of the National Savings Bank were so stupid and pettifogging, only supporters of the Labour Party, who evidently had more time and patience than sense, would be likely to patronise it.

The reasoning may be illogical, and unfair to the Post Office, which has to protect itself and the public against fraud, but this kind of emotional response is a fact of the political situation. It is just as real as cheering or booing at a meeting and a Government which pays no attention to it is blind to its best interests. One of the main functions of an efficient Public Relations Department is to keep the Ministry or the Government aware of situations which are not working to its advantage, in the hope that by removing the causes of dissatisfaction and irritation, hostile feelings can be nipped in the bud. To think only of the Post Office, an institution which affects most people directly, there can be little doubt, firstly, that most people consider it inefficient and, secondly, that any increase in its efficiency would cause the electorate to think more favourable of any Government which happened to be in power at the time. The sad truth, however, is that Governments expect their public relations staff to perform miracles with what exists, not to benefit from what might and should exist. This is why so much, perhaps most official public relations is a waste of time and money, since it is concerned with selling or trying to sell goods which the public knows to be unsatisfactory.

There is an important difference between political public relations in Britain and America. In Britain what we are pleased to call our public life is conducted in a much more private and secret fashion than in any other democratic country. As one of our most experienced political analysts once said:

> Our politicians and civil servants, the public men, the "insiders" who govern us, have their own way of running affairs in which

they accord only a small part to the press. Anybody who is anybody has access to almost anybody else who is anybody without the need for the intermediacy of the press. . . . The path to the top in British politics does not lie in adroit self-publicising or in winning the good-will of journalists by slight indiscretions. It depends upon impressing one's party leader.'[10]

This creates a gap between the inner governing group and the electorate which cannot be bridged adequately by handouts or organised public relations, or by any talk of 'being frank with the country'. There is a 'we' and 'they' atmosphere about British politics, no matter which Party is in power, which is quite different from what one finds in America, and which often gives the Government's marketing of itself a certain patronising quality. There are those who would sooner be persuaded than patronised.

Notes

Notes to Chapter 1

1. Transcript of an interview with David Dimbleby, published in *The Listener*, 27th March, 1975. *The Listener* is an unequalled source of material for anyone wishing to study the extempore remarks of politicians and other public figures. No other country provides this kind of week-by-week service of transcripts of broadcast discussions and interviews, and for this reason no apology is required for the number of quotations from *The Listener* which are included in the present book.
2. *A Dictionary of Political Analysis*, Longman, 1971.
3. 'The Intellectual Error of Communism', *World Review*, March, 1950, p. 42.
4. Sir Ian expresses this view in his political testament, *Inside Right*, published in 1977.
5. 'Propaganda without theory', *The Spectator*, 15th October, 1977.
6. 'Truth at last, but what if it is too late?', *The Times*, 29th September, 1976.
7. K. R. Minogue, *The Liberal Mind*, Methuen, 1963, p. 13.
8. *The New Language of Politics: an anecdotal dictionary of catchwords, slogans and political usage*, New York: Random House, 1968.
9. *The Liberal Mind*, p. 99.
10. Colin Brogan, *Our New Masters*, Hollis and Carter, 1947, p. 11.
11. 'The Architecture of Ideology: Style and Dogma', in *The Struggle for Europe*, Contact Books, 1948.

Notes to Chapter 2

1. Christopher Johnson, 'Tweedledum and Tweedledee', *The Listener*, 30th September, 1976.
2. *TUC Report*, 1972, p. 432.
3. *TUC Report*, 1967, p. 461.
4. November/December, 1977. It is an official Communist Party publication.
5. Stanley Kelly, Jr. *Professional Public Relations and Political Power* Baltimore: The Johns Hopkins Press, 1956, p. 50.
6. On this, see Jay G. Blumler and Denis McQuail, *Television in Politics: its Uses and Influences*, Faber, 1969, and Krishnan Kumar, 'The Political Consequences of Television', *The Listener*, 3rd July, 1969.
7. *The Listener*, 5th October, 1967.
8. Hearings before the Select Committee on Presidential Campaign Activities of the United States Senate, 93rd Congress, First Session: Watergate and Related Activities.

Phase I: Watergate Investigation. Washington DC, May 17, 18, 22, 23 and 24, 1973, Book 1, pp. 364–365.

Notes to Chapter 3

1. Article by him, 'Office before Honour', *The Spectator*, 15th October, 1977.
2. Westport, Conn: Greenwood Press, 1959, pp. 14–15.
3. In his book, *Dirty Politics*, a history of 'dirty campaigning and political chicanery in America', New York: W. W. Norton and Co., 1966.
4. Felknor, p. 128.
5. Paul T. David, et al., *The Politics of National Party Conventions*, The Brookings Institution, 1960, p. 305.
6. Alistair Cooke, 'Carter Cools the Gospel', *The Listener*, 19th May, 1977.
7. Keith Kyle, 'The Laughter and the Tears', *The Listener*, 27th January, 1977.
8. Michael Wood, 'Alibis ad lib', *New Society*, 22nd April, 1976.
9. BBC radio interview with Leslie Smith, *The Listener*, 13th March, 1969.
10. Andrew Alexander and Alan Watkins, *The Making of the Prime Minister*, Macdonald, 1970.
11. Quoted in full in Harold Wilson, *The Labour Government, 1964–70*, Weidenfeld/Michael Joseph, 1971, p. 69.
12. *The Listener*, 26th June, 1969.
13. Keith Graves, *The Listener*, 10th October, 1974.
14. On this, see Margaret Laing, *Edward Heath: Prime Minister*, Sidgwick & Jackson, 1972. She says: ' "He is like a computer. Feed it with information and all you have to do is to wait for the answer", says one Cabinet colleague. It is a simile often applied to him.'
15. Interview with Robin Day, *The Listener*, 31st January, 1974.
16. Patrick Cosgrave, 'Our New Prime Minister', *Daily Telegraph*, 6th April, 1976.
17. Ibid.
18. *New Society*, 22nd April, 1976.
19. 18th December, 1976.
20. *Hansard*, 1st April, 1968.
21. 23rd March, 1961.
22. 10th April, 1962.
23. Second Inaugural Address.
24. Speech at the University of Michigan, 22nd May, 1964.
25. 'A politician's word', *The Listener*, 13th June, 1974.

Notes to Chapter 4

1. 'Demeaning of Meaning', in Neil Postman et al., *Language in America*, New York: Pegasus, 1969.
2. *TUC Report*, 1972, p. 427.
3. Ibid, p. 428.
4. Ibid.
5. *TUC Report*, 1972, p. 433.
6. Ibid.

7. *Labour Party Conference Report*, 1968, p. 147.
8. *TUC Report*, 1967, p. 532.
9. *Link International*. Published by the Trade Union Committee for International Co-operation and Development, September/October, 1977.
10. *Socialist Worker*, 8th October, 1977.
11. *Challenge*, 'Paper of the Young Communist League', November/December, 1977.
12. *93rd Conservative Conference, Brighton, 1976, Verbatim Report*, p. 126.
13. Ibid, p. 83.
14. Ibid, p. 76.
15. Ibid, p. 23.
16. Reported in *Conservative Monthly News*, November, 1977, under the headline, 'Tentacles of Union Power'.
17. *Political Adventure: the Memoirs of the Earl of Kilmuir*, Weidenfeld and Nicolson, 1964, p. 271.
18. Ibid, p. 327.
19. *Hansard*, 13th March, 1967.
20. *Hansard*, 5th May, 1972.
21. *The Diplomatic Career*, André Deutsch, 1962, pp. 61–2.
22. Ibid, p. 64.
23. Dr. David Owen, 'What next in Africa', *The Listener*, 8th December, 1977.
24. Sir Cecil Parrott, 'Foreign Secretaries', *The Listener*, 18th April, 1968. Sir Cecil was formerly British Minister to Moscow and Ambassador to Czechoslovakia.
25. Ibid.

Notes to Chapter 5

1. *The Listener*, 11th July, 1974.
2. 'Politics and the English Language'. Reprinted in *The Collected Essays, Journalism and Letters of George Orwell*, Vol. IV, Secker and Warburg, 1968, p. 129.
3. 'As I Please', originally printed in *Tribune*, 17th March, 1944 and reproduced in *The Collected Essays*, Vol. III, pp. 110–111.
4. Bert Ramelson, 'The Crisis and the Way Out', *Morning Star*, 21st January, 1978.
5. *Comment: Communist Fortnightly Review*, 29th November, 1975.
6. Betty Matthews, *Britain and the Socialist Revolution*, London, 1975.
7. Ibid.
8. *Comment*, 29th November, 1975.
9. *Comment*, 29th November, 1975.
10. C. Mullard, *Black Britain*, Inscape Corporation, 1973.
11. Seymour Martin Lipset, *Rebellion in the University*, Boston: Little, Brown and Co., 1971.
12. Betty Matthews, op. cit.
13. *Morning Star*, 20th February, 1976.
14. *Comment*, 11th November, 1975.
15. David Rubinstein and Colin Stoneman (eds.), *Education for Democracy*, Penguin Books, 1970.

16. Bruce L. Felknor, *Dirty Politics*, New York: W. W. Norton, 1966, p. 99.
17. *Shepton Mallet Journal*, 19th January, 1978.
18. *Our New Masters*, Hollis and Carter, 1947.
19. Ibid, p. 69.
20. *Hansard*, 25th March, 1977. Debate on the European Parliament.
21. Ibid.
22. *Hansard*, 23rd March, 1977.
23. *Hansard*, 31st March, 1977.
24. Jonathan Sumption, 'Liberty, equality, hypocrisy', *Sunday Telegraph*, 18th December, 1977.
25. The well-known professional revolutionary, who came to public notice during the student unrest of the 1960s.
26. *Hansard*, 4th April, 1968.
27. 'Office before honour', *The Spectator*, 15th October, 1977.
28. Brian Walden, 'After Prentice, who next?', *The Spectator*, 15th October, 1977.
29. K. Daly, *93rd Conservative Conference, Brighton, 1976, Verbatim Report*, p. 51.
30. Ibid, p. 52.
31. On Radio Clyde, 27th October, 1977.

Notes to Chapter 6

1. *The Times*, 23rd January, 1978.
2. Interview with Anthony King, *The Listener*, 5th September, 1974.
3. Anthony Barker and Michael Rush, *The Member of Parliament and his Information*, Allen and Unwin, 1970.
4. Ibid, p. 35.
5. *The Listener*, 15th August, 1974. Television interview by Anthony King.
6. *The Listener*, 11th August, 1977. Television interview by Anthony King.
7. 'Lord Avon reminisces', *The Listener*, 13th January, 1977. Television interview with Kenneth Harris.
8. Geoffrey McDermott, *The Eden Legacy and the Decline of British Diplomacy*, Leslie Frewin, 1969, p. 19.
9. *The Listener*, 9th June, 1977. Television interview with Michael Charlton.
10. *The Listener*, 8th June, 1967. Television interview with Kenneth Harris.
11. *The Listener*, 8th August, 1974. Radio interview with Nicholas Woolley.
12. *The Listener*, 23rd January, 1969. Television interview.
13. *Congressional Record*, Senate, 4th June, 1968.
14. *Hansard*, 13th March, 1967.
15. *Congressional Record*, Senate, 23rd May, 1968.
16. Ibid.
17. *U.S. Congress, Senate, Permanent Sub-Committee on Investigations of Committee on Government Operations*, 83rd Congress, 2nd Session, 1954, pp. 52–53.
18. *Transcripts of Eight Recorded Presidential Conversations. Hearings before the Committee on the Judiciary, House of Representatives*. 93rd Congress, Second Session, May–June 1974, pp. 190–191.

Notes to Chapter 7

1. The substance of this chapter appeared as an article, 'The Last Chink in their Armour', published in *Encounter*, March, 1976.
2. Andrew Roth *Heath and the Heathmen* Routledge & Kegan Paul, 1972, p. 2.
3. Printed in *The Listener*, 18th September, 1969.
4. Frances Lloyd George, *The Years That Are Past*, Hutchinson, 1967, p. 159.
5. Thomas Jones, *Lloyd George*, Oxford University Press, 1967.
6. *93rd Conservative Conference, 1976, Verbatim Report*, p. 137.
7. 'To Dafydd life was a battle and he was never happy unless he had somebody or something to fight.' William George, *My Brother and I*, Eyre and Spottiswood, 1958.
8. *Chips: The Diary of Sir Henry Cannon*, Weidenfeld and Nicolson, 1967, p. 327.
9. Notably by A. J. P. Taylor and others in *Churchill: Four Faces and the Man*, and by Brian Gardner, *Churchill in His Time*. Two of the contributions, by Anthony Storr ('The Man') and Robert Rhodes James ('The Politician') are especially valuable.
10. 'He projected a style and polish to the business of governing, maintaining a fastidious dislike of officialese and jargon of all kinds . . . I marvelled at his extraordinary application. Nothing was too much trouble. Every sentence was written and rewritten; every quotation was checked; every phrase weighed in the balance.' (Harold Macmillan, *Tides of Fortune*, Macmillan, 1969)
11. 'The nose of the bulldog has been slanted backwards, so that he can breathe without letting go.'
12. Taylor, op. cit., pp. 239–240.
13. *The Roar of the Lion*, Allan Wingate-Baker, 1969.
14. In *Edward Heath: Prime Minister*, Sidgwick and Jackson, 1972, p. 25.
15. The phrase is Lord Avon's own.
16. Randolph Churchill, *The Rise and Fall of Sir Anthony Eden*, MacGibbon and Kee, 1959, p. 17.
17. Ibid, p. 43.
18. L. MacNeil Weir, *The Tragedy of Ramsay MacDonald*, Secker and Warburg, 1948.

Notes to Chapter 8

1. 'How to tell the people: a discussion on the British Government's public relations', *The Changing Nation*, Contact Books, 1947.
2. Ibid.
3. Leaflet, *New Pensions: National Insurance Contributions*. Issued by the Department of Health and Social Security, 1978.
4. Labour Party election material, 1972.
5. 'The Public Progress', in a Contact Book of that name, 1947.
6. Richard Rose (ed.), *Politics in England Today*, Faber, 1974.
7. Walburga von Raffler-Engel, 'We do not talk only with our mouths', *Verbatim: the Language Quarterly*, Vol. IV, No. 3, December, 1977, p. 1.
8. Hugh Clayton, 28th January, 1978.
9. July, 1977.
10. David Butler, 'Political Reporting in Britain', *The Listener*, 15th August, 1963.

Books Found Useful

There are innumerable books about politics and politicians and very nearly as many about the English language but, for some curious reason, remarkably little has been written about the language of politics. After thirty years, there is still nothing to equal what George Orwell had to say on the subject in *The English People* (Collins, 1947) and in his article for *Tribune* (14th March 1944), which concentrated on the Communist jargon. The article, 'Propaganda and Democratic Speech', which was published in *Partisan Review* (Summer 1944) is also very good and has stood up to the passage of time remarkably well. So, too, has the famous essay, 'Politics and the English Language' (*Horizon*, April 1946). Orwell was able to bring politics and language within the same focus because he was not crippled by the limitations of the specialist in either field. He wrote what he felt he had to write, ignoring the traditional academic boundaries between 'subjects'. Subsequent academics were able to praise him, especially when he was safely dead, but their professional reputation would not allow them to imitate him. The study of language has gone in one direction, the study of politics in another, and the regrettable lack of a bridge between them has prevented a form of analysis of which both politicians and politics have stood in urgent and serious need. One can search in vain for Orwell-type contributions to the leading British and American journals devoted to politics – *Political Quarterly, American Political Science Review, British Journal of Political Science, Political Studies* and, most serious gap of all, *Teaching Politics*, the Journal of the Politics Association – and with equal lack of success in the periodicals which are concerned with language and language teaching.

The books listed below are mentioned here, not because they deal in any way comprehensively with the subject of Orwell's essays and of the present book, but because they may have been found to contain information and ideas which suggest how the language of politics can be properly explored.

THE PRACTICE AND ART OF POLITICS

Blondel, Jean, *Voters, Parties and Leaders: the Social Fabric of British Politics*, Revised ed., Penguin Books, 1977
Brett, Lionel et al., *The Struggle for Power*, Contact Books, 1948
David, Paul T. et al., *The Politics of National Party Conventions*, The Brookings Institution, 1960
Duverges, M., *The Idea of Politics*, Methuen, 1966
Felknor, Bruce L., *Dirty Politics*, New York: W. W. Norton, 1966
Hodgson, Godfrey, *In Our Time: America from World War II to Nixon*, Macmillan, 1977
Information and the Public Interest, HMSO, 1969
Kelly, Stanley, Jr., *Professional Public Relations and Political Power*, Baltimore: Johns Hopkins Press, 1956
Mackintosh, John P., *The Government and Politics of Britain*, 4th ed., Hutchinson, 1977
McGinniss, Joe, *The Selling of the President*, Deutsch, 1970
Mayhew, Christopher, *Party Games*, Hutchinson, 1969
Miller, J. D. B., *The Nature of Politics*, Penguin Books, 1965
Minogue, K. R., *The Liberal Mind*, Methuen, 1963
Richards, P. G., *Honourable Member*, 2nd ed., Faber, 1964
Roberts, Geoffrey K., *A Dictionary of Political Analysis*, Longman, 1971
Rose, Richard (ed.), *Politics in England Today*, Faber, 1974
Rose, Richard (ed.), *Studies in British Politics*, 2nd ed., Macmillan, 1965
Sampson, Anthony, *The New Anatomy of Britain*, Hodder, 1971
Strang, Lord, *The Diplomatic Career*, Deutsch, 1962
Warner, W. Lloyd, *The Living and the Dead: a Study of the Symbolic Life of Americans*, Westport, Conn.: Greenwood Press, 1959
Williams, David, *Not in the Public Interest*, Hutchinson, 1965

POLITICS, LANGUAGE AND THE MEDIA

Barker, Anthony and Rush, Michael, *The Member of Parliament and his Information*, Allen and Unwin, 1970
Blumler, Jay G. and McQuail, Denis, *Television in Politics: its Uses and Influence*, Faber, 1968
Hughes, Emrys, *Parliament and Mumbo Jumbo*, Allen and Unwin, 1966

Postman, Neil, et al., *Language in America*, New York: Pegasus, 1965
Roberts, Godfrey K., *A Dictionary of Political Analysis*, Longman, 1971
Safire, William, *The New Language of Politics: an anecdotal dictionary of catchwords, slogans and political usage*, New York: Random House, 1968
Trenaman, J. and McQuail, D., *Television and the Public Image*, Methuen, 1961
Windlesham, Lord, *Communication and Political Power*, Cape, 1966

INDIVIDUALS IN THE WORLD OF POLITICS

Attlee, C. R., *As It Happened*, Heinemann, 1954
Avon, Earl of, *The Eden Memoirs: Facing the Dictators*, Cassell, 1962
Avon, Earl of, *The Eden Memoirs: The Reckoning*, Cassell, 1965
Bell, Jack, *The Johnson Treatment. How Lyndon B. Johnson took over the Presidency and made it his own*, New York: Harper and Row, 1965
Butler, Lord, *The Art of the Possible*, Penguin Books, 1973
Churchill, Randolph, *The Rise and Fall of Sir Anthony Eden*, MacGibbon and Kee, 1959
Crossman, Richard, *The Diaries of a Cabinet Minister*, 3 vols., Hamish Hamilton/Jonathan Cape, 1976-77
Dalton, Hugh, *High Tide and After*, Muller, 1962
Feiling, Keith, *The Life of Neville Chamberlain*, Macmillan, 1946
Hutchinson, George, *Edward Heath: a Personal and Political Biography*, Longman, 1970
Hyde, H. Montgomery, *Baldwin: the Unexpected Prime Minister*, Hart-Davis/MacGibbon and Kee, 1973
James, Robert Rhodes (ed.), *Chips: the Diaries of Sir Henry Channon*, Weidenfeld and Nicolson, 1967
Kilmuir, Earl of, *Political Adventure: the Memoirs of the Earl of Kilmuir*, Weidenfeld and Nicolson, 1964
Laing, Margaret, *Edward Heath, Prime Minister*, Sidgwick and Jackson, 1972
Lyttelton, Oliver (Viscount Chandos), *The Memoirs of Lord Chandos*, Bodley Head, 1962
Macmillan, Harold, *Winds of Change* and the succeeding 6 volumes of his autobiography, Macmillan, 1966-77
Roth, Andrew, *Heath and the Heathmen*, Routledge and Kegan Paul, 1972

Sylvester, A. J., *The Real Lloyd George*, Cassell, 1947
Taylor, A. J. P., *Churchill: Four Faces and the Man*, Allen Lane, 1969
Weir, L. MacNeill, *The Tragedy of Ramsay MacDonald*, Secker and Warburg, 1938
Wilson, Harold, *The Labour Government, 1964–70*, Weidenfeld Michael Joseph, 1971

Index

abuse, in politics, 82–101
academics, and politics, 3
accents, 52–3
addiction to politics, 18
adversary politics, 22–3
Advertising Code, 28
Agricultural Mortgage Corporation, 107
Agriculture, Ministry of, 149, 150
Alexander, Alan, 155
American elections, 32
American way of life, 15
analysts of politics, 9
architecture as form of political language, 19
Argentina, 12
Attlee, Lord, 139
attractions of political life, 39–40
audiences, politicians' love of, 16
Avon, Lord, 109, 135–7
avuncular image, 44–5

Baker, Senator, 37–8
Baldwin, Lord, 138–9, 140
Barker, Anthony, 157
Barker, Captain, 37–8
Bell, Tom, 68
Benn, Anthony Wedgwood, 28, 33, 34–5, 52, 64
Black Britain, 156
'blackmail', 67
Blumler, Jay G., 154
boredom in politics, 17
'both sides of industry', 23–4
bourgeois ideals, 19
Brett, Lionel, 19–20
Brewster, Senator, 117
Briginshaw, R., 23, 63–4
Britain and the Socialist Revolution, 156
British Leyland, 66–7

Brogan, Colin, 92–4
Brook, Gerald, 97
Brookings Institution, 46
Brown, Rosemary, 71–2
Buchan, Norman, 101
business interests, 14
Butler, David, 158

Callaghan, James, 48, 52, 56–7, 100, 107, 110, 128
capitalism, 4
Carter, President, 47–8
Castle, Barbara, 8–9, 64, 96
causes, 14
Central Office of Information, 141–2
Challenge, 26–7
Chandos, Lord, 110
character assassination, 45
child labour, 15
Chips: The Diaries of Sir Henry Cannon, 158
Churchill, Randolph, 137
Churchill, Sir Winston, 48–9, 109, 129–31
Churchill: Four Faces and the Man, 158
Clayton, Hugh, 158
clichés, 15
closed shop, 14
colour-coding of political candidates, 28–9
Comment, 156
Commonwealth Prime Ministers' Conference, 114, 115
Communism, 4, 7–8
Communist language, 65–8, 84–7, 130
competition, 6
comprehensive schools, 28
Congressional Record, 104
Congressmen, 14, 19
Conservatism, 6, 8
Conservative Central Office, 141

Index

Conservative language, 70–3
Conservative Monthly News, 156
Conservative Party Conference, 71–2
Conservative politics, natural as breathing, 1
Cooke, Alistair, 155
Cooke, Robert, 31
Cooper, Jack, 64
Corn Laws, 15
Cosgrave, Patrick, 56
Cousins, Frank, 64
Crossman, Richard, 33, 95–6

Daly, K., 157
David, Paul T., 156
Day, Robin, 9, 12, 53–4, 114
Dean, John, 120–1
death penalty, 15
deceit, 12, 16–17
definition of politics, 2–4
Democratic Party, 46
dictatorship, Communist theory of, 8
Dictionary of Political Analysis, A, 154
Dimbleby, David, 154
Diplomatic Career, The, 156
diplomatic language, 78–81
dirty politics, 45
doctrinaires, 15
Dodd, Senator, 114–15
dogma, 13, 14, 19
Don't Knows, 145, 146
Douglas-Home, Sir Alec, 139
Draughtsmen's and Allied Technicians' Association, 24
drinking among politicians, 8

Eden, Sir Anthony, 109–10, 135–7
Education for Democracy, 150
Edward Heath, Prime Minister, 155, 158
election addresses, 29–31, 34–5, 42–3
Empire Marketing Board, 142, 143
Encounter, 158
envy, 6, 8
equality of opportunity, 15
evasiveness, 57
Exemptions from Ingredient Listing, 149

face, loss of political, 13
factual information as propaganda, 43

Fair Campaign Practices Committee, 45
families of politicians, 31
Family Allowances and National Insurance Bill, 22
fanatics, 15
fantasy world of politicians, 13
Fascism, 7
Felknor, Bruce, 45
fighting-cocks, politicians as, 33
Fletcher, Raymond, 57
folk heroes, 44
Food Standards Committee, 151
Forte, Sir Charles, 96
Fraser, Sir Robert, 141
fraud, 12

Gardner, Brian, 158
General Medical Council, 17
General Strike, 1929, 1
George, William, 158
George-Brown, Lord, 2–3, 8, 9, 80–1, 134
Gilmour, Sir Ian, 8
Golding, J., 77
Goodman, Lord, 77
grand style, 48–9, 50–1
greed, 6
Griffiths, Eldon, 22–3
gun lobby, 115

handouts from Government departments, 144–5
Hansard, 22, 78, 104
Harris, Kenneth, 157
Harrisson, Tom, 145
Hart, Judith, 56–7
Healey, Denis, 10–11, 100
Heath, Edward, 26–7, 30, 49, 52–3, 54–5, 96, 122–3, 135, 140
Heath and the Heathmen, 158
Heffer, Eric, 95
Hitler, Adolf, 140
homosexuals, 15
Hoover, J. Edgar, 38
House of Commons style, 76–7, 94–5
human nature, politicians' view of, 5–6
Humphrey, Senator Hubert, 47–8
Hunt, Senator, 38

Index

idealism, 14
ideologies, 13, 62
Industrial Relations Act, 62
Inland Revenue, 25
inner dignity, 48
insensitivity, 54
Inside Right, 154
intellectuals in politics, 8
Iremonger, T. R., 97

jargon, 10, 68
Jay, Peter, 52
Jenkins, Roy, 23, 43
Johnson, Christopher, 154
Johnson, President, 57, 111
Jones, Thomas, 158
Joseph, Sir Keith, 95
journalists, 9–12

Kaufman, G. B., 77
Kelly, Stanley, 154
Kennedy, Jacqueline, 112
Kennedy, President John F., 48–9, 58–9, 111, 112
Kilmuir, Lord, 73, 74
Kipling, Rudyard, 105, 143
Kyle, Keith, 155

Labour Government, 1964–70, The, 155
Labour Party, 14
Labour Party Conference, 70
Laing, Margaret, 155
Language in America, 155
Laos, 58–9
Law, Bonar, 139
leadership, 47–8
Lenin, 8
Levin, Bernard, 10–12
Lewis, Arthur, 22
Liberal Mind, The, 154
Liberals, an embarrassment in adversary politics, 33
liberal tradition, 13–14
Link International, 156
Listener, The, 154, 155, 156
Living and the Dead, The, 44
Lloyd George, David, 125–9
Lloyd George, Frances, 158

lying, 12
Lynch, Jack, 48

McCall, James, 116
McCarthy, Senator, 119
McCarthy witchhunts, 88
MacDonald, Ramsay, 112, 132, 137–8
McGahey, M., 55
McGarvey, Dan, 64
McKinnon, Judge, 90–1
Mackintosh, John P., 103
Macmillan, Harold, 48, 52, 110, 131–4, 139
McQuail, Denis, 154
Making of the Prime Minister, The, 155
managed news, 57
manifestos, 5
marketing in politics, 21, 28–9; in Trade Unionism, 23–4
Marx, Karl, 4, 132
Marxism, 4, 7
Marxist phraseology, 84–7
Marylebone Cricket Club, 17
Matthews, Betty, 156
Mellish, Bob, 100
Member of Parliament and his Information, The, 157
Members of Parliament, 14–15
metaphors as clue to politicians' minds, 124–40
middlemen in politics, 9–10
Minogue, K. R., 12–13, 16–17
morality, 13–14
Morning Star, 85, 156
Morrison, Senator Cameron, 88
Morrison, Herbert, 8, 93–4
motivation, 6, 8
mudslinging, 45
Mullard, C., 156
Mulley, Fred, 57
My Brother and I, 158

National Enterprise Board, 66
National Front, 82
National Rifle Association, 115
National Savings for You, 151
National Shooting Sports Federation, 115
National Society of Operative Printers, 23, 63

National Union of Agricultural and Allied Workers, 66
National Union of General and Municipal Workers, 65
National Union of Miners, 55
New Language of Politics, The, 154
news conferences, 58–9
New Society, 155
New York Times, 45
Nineteen Eighty Four, 117
nit-picking, 36
Nixon, President Richard M., 41, 48, 59, 112, 120–1, 140
Not Officer Class, 51–2

'obscene', 83–7
occupations of political candidates, 28
'Office before Honour', 41
Oral Answers in House of Commons, 57
oratory, 48–52
Orwell, George, 10, 84–5, 117
Our New Masters, 92
Owen, Dr. David 107, 110
Oxford English Dictionary, 2, 5, 82, 84, 96

Page, W., 66
Palmer, Arthur, 29–31
Parliament Chamber, effect on speaking style, 76
party conferences, 35
party conventions in United States, 46
Peart, Lord, 107
Philip, Prince, 101
poets, rare among politicians, 19
Political Adventure, 156
political analysts, 9
political animals, 9, 17–18
political drama, 47–8
political journalists, 9–12
political middlemen, 9–10
political principles, 8, 34–5, 43
Politics in England Today, 5
Politics of National Party Conventions, The, 155
Postman, Neil, 61
Post Office, 142–3
Powell, Enoch, 41–2, 98–9
power, 7–8, 12, 39–60
Prentice, Reg, 99–100

primary audience for broadcasts, 46
privilege, 7–8
product differentiation in politics, 21–2, 26–8
Professional Public Relations and Political Power, 154
programmes of the political parties, 5
promises, 42, 50
pseudo-frankness, 113–14
pseudo-intimacy, 113
public image of politicians, 13, 44–5, 46
Public Relations Society of America, 32
public spirit, 14
puppets in politics, 29
Pym, Francis, 94

'racism', 88, 89–90
Raffler-Engel, Walburga von, 158
Ramelson, Bert, 156
redistribution of wealth, 15
resignations, 41
Reynolds, Senator Robert R., 88
Rhodes James, Robert, 158
Rise and Fall of Sir Anthony Eden, The, 158
Roberts, Geoffrey K., 3–5
Rockefeller, Governor, 46
Rose, Richard, 5, 147
Roth, Andrew, 158
Rubinstein, David, 156
Rush, Michael, 157
Rusk, Dean, 111
Russell, Bertrand, 7–8

Safire, William, 16
Salinger, Pierre, 58
Salisbury, Lord, 73
Savings Bank, 152
Scanlon, Hugh, 62–3
screen-battles, 32–3
secondary audience for broadcasts, 46–7
sectional interests, 14
self-employed, 24–6
Senate hearings, 38
Shakespeare, William, 140
Shepton Mallet Journal, 157
Shinwell, Emanuel, 112
slavery, 15
slogans, 59–60

Smith, Leslie, 123
Socialism, 4, 6
Socialist Worker, 156
social justice, 15
South Africa, 12
Soviet Union, 7, 12
Spectator, The, 8–9, 154, 156
speechwriters, 49, 124, 125
Spurgeon, Caroline, 139, 140
staffs of Senators, 41
status-anxiety, 7
Stoneman, Colin, 156
Storr, Anthony, 158
Strang, Lord, 78
Street Offences Act, 26
Struggle for Europe, The, 154
Summerskill, Dr., 75
Sumption, Jonathan, 157
Sunday Telegraph, 96
Sutherland, Graham, 129
Swift, Jonathan, 10
Sylvester, Arthur, 57

Tallents, Sir Stephen, 142–3
Tariq Ali, 87, 97
taxation, 31
Taylor, A. J. P., 158
telephone tapping, 117
television, influence on political style, 33–4; presentation of politics in America, 36
television interviewers, 9
television producers, fondness for adversary politics, 32–3
Thatcher, Margaret, 52–3, 105, 106
Thorpe, Jeremy, 94
thumbprints, 68–70
Times, The, 10, 97, 149–50, 154
Tower, Senator, 118
Trade Unions, 14
Trades Descriptions Act, 28, 148

Trades Union Congress, 23, 50, 62–5, 70
Tragedy of Ramsay MacDonald, The, 158
transcripts, misleading nature of, 47
Transport House, 141
Tribune, 150
Truman, President, 59

values in politics, 12
Veitch, Miss, 65
Verbatim, 158
vested interests, 14
Vietnam, 15, 58
voting habits, 43–4

Walden, Brian, 157
Ward, Irene, 75
Warner, Lloyd, 44
Washington Post, 12
Watergate, 38
Watkins, Alan, 8–9, 155
Watt, David, 60, 82–4
Weir, L. McNeil, 158
West, Richard, 35, 36
Whitaker, Clem, 32
Wilkins, W. A., 75
Williams, Shirley, 28
Wilson, Sir Harold, 19, 48, 49–50, 54–5, 96, 103, 112, 113–14, 133–5, 140
Winterbottom, W. E., 24–6
wire tapping, 117
wives of politicians, 31
Women's Institutes, 1, 3
Wood, Michael, 56–7
World Review, 154

Years that Are Past, The, 158
Yeats, W. B., 105
Young Communist League, 69

Zwicker, General Ralph, 119